SILENCING
THE ENEMY

WITH PRAISE

ROBERT GAY

SILENCING THE ENEMY WITH PRAISE
by Robert Gay

ISBN -13: 978-1-60273-005-2
ISBN -10: 1-60273-005-9
Library of Congress Control Number: 2010924727

Printed in the United States of America.
For World-Wide Distribution.

This is a revised, updated, and expanded edition of the book published in 1993 under the title *Silencing the Enemy*.

Parsons Publishing House
P. O. Box 488
Stafford, VA 22554 USA
www.ParsonsPublishingHouse.com
Info@ParsonsPublishingHouse.com

Cover & Graphic Art by Micah Gay.

TABLE OF CONTENTS

DEDICATION

This book is dedicated especially to my wife, Stacey, and our three children who are all serving the Lord today and actively participating in ministry. I am truly a man that is blessed beyond that of worldly possessions and will forever be grateful for you. I love you with all of my heart.

I also want to express my sincere appreciation for my parents who taught me the way of the Lord from the time I was born. You have always been faithful to the Lord and to our family. God's greatest blessings will be revealed for the seeds you have sown.

I want to express a special word of thanks to Bishop and Mom Hamon, my spiritual parents, who have labored in the kingdom of God for over fifty years. Your encouragement and support over the years has been invaluable. Thank you for the example that you have set for others to follow.

I also want to communicate a word of gratitude to our church family of High Praise Worship Center in Panama City, Florida. All of you are awesome. You have all been such a blessing to our family through the years.

Finally, I want to give thanks to the Lord Jesus for His grace and love that He has poured out upon us all. The greatest privilege of all is to be a part of the family of God. Thank You, Lord.

FOREWORD

This book was originally published in 1993 under the title *Silencing the Enemy*. After seventeen years in print, it is now being released in an expanded form under the title *Silencing the Enemy With Praise*. Much of the original material has been edited and brought up to date along with approximately one fourth of the book being brand new material.

It is the desire of this author for this book to be a resource for you in your Christian walk and enlighten you to the power of praise and worship. Worship teams will be able to derive understandings which will further their worship ministry in the local church. This book offers a wealth of information and revelation concerning praise as a weapon of spiritual warfare. It is our prayer that it be a blessing to you.

Darrell J. Parsons
Parsons Publishing House

THE EVOLUTION OF PRAISE AND WORSHIP

Music and worship have played an integral role in the church throughout history. A study of church music and worship reveals that God has restored different elements of worship progressively. He has led the church from glory to glory through fresh revelation from heaven. As the church was changed and conformed to what God was saying in times past, so we must change and conform to what He is saying today.

God uses a person to proclaim the revelation which the Holy Spirit is illuminating to the church. The unfolding of this revelation to the body of Christ becomes known as a restorational move of God. Paralleling this, He also raises up psalmists to write songs that embody the truths of that movement. Thus, He enhances every movement through the use of music and worship.

An in-depth study of church history also illustrates that with every move of God came changes in the way worship was expressed. Along with new songs, other expressions of worship became more demonstrative. Musical instruments that were considered "taboo" by a previous generation were brought into the church.

The church in recent years has seen a tremendous growth in the emphasis of praise and worship. More CDs, books, seminars and manuals have been produced on this subject in the last three decades than in the entire history of the church.

All this activity indicates that once again the wind of the Spirit is blowing throughout the earth to usher in fresh insight, revelation and experiences, accompanied by new songs, choruses and expressions of worship. Distinct emphasis on particular aspects of praise and worship will take us to a higher realm of glory and a new experience with God. He has prepared new garments for us to wear in our generation. The Spirit of God is bidding us to come up a little higher.

Today a fresh sound is coming forth. God is raising up men and women who are writing songs to bring the church to attention. These songs are teaching and admonishing us with the truths concerning spiritual warfare. God is raising up prophetic songwriters to bring forth songs of spiritual warfare so the church may become the spiritual army He has called it to be.

Jesus said that His church would be built upon the rock (Matt. 16:18). He went on to say that as the church is built upon that rock, the gates of Hell will not prevail against it. The ministry of praise and worship must be built upon a rock of revelation-knowledge.

The Bible says that the people of God are destroyed for a lack of knowledge (Hos. 4:6). Without a revelation of what God is saying concerning worship in this hour, we will be like the children of Israel who wandered in the wilderness for forty years and died. But, as we joyfully receive and enter into the revelation of the Spirit, we will be like those who crossed the Jordan and obtained their promised possession. Let us not be a generation of wilderness walkers but rather Canaan conquerors!

Our praise is a weapon of spiritual warfare. God has a prophetic purpose for establishing praise and worship in the church. As you read and study this book, allow the Holy Spirit to birth the truths contained here in your heart. As you do, I believe your life will be changed.

CHAPTER ONE

GOD'S PROPHETIC PURPOSE FOR PRAISE

Amos prophesied by the Spirit about a time when God would restore the tabernacle of David.

> *In that day I will restore David's fallen tent. I will repair its broken places, restore its ruins, and build it as it used to be, so that they may possess* (Amos 9:11-12, NIV).

David's fallen tent refers to what is more commonly known as the tabernacle of David. Let me define briefly what that constituted.

In 1 Chronicles chapter sixteen, we read the account of the origin of David's tabernacle. We can see from Scripture that this was a place of praise. Inside David's tabernacle was the Ark of the Covenant, and before the ark the priests gave continual praise, worship and thanks. It was a place of joy where music resounded in honor of Jehovah God.

1

> *They brought the ark of God and set it*
> *inside the tent that David had pitched*
> *for it, and they presented burnt offer-*
> *ings before God... He appointed some*
> *of the Levites to minister before the*
> *ark of the Lord, to make petition, to*
> *give thanks, and to praise the Lord, the*
> *God of Israel: Asaph was the chief,*
> *Zechariah   second,   then   Jeiel,*
> *Shemiramoth, Jehiel, Mattithiah, Eliab,*
> *Benaiah, Obed-Edom and Jeiel. They*
> *were to play the lyres and harps. Asaph*
> *was to sound the cymbals, and Benaiah*
> *and Jahaziel the priests were to blow*
> *the trumpets regularly before the ark*
> *of the covenant of God* (1 Chr. 16:1, 4-
> 6, NIV).

We can easily see that the tabernacle of David was a place where God was continually praised and worshipped. In the Old Testament it was the ultimate place of worship – a place of continual praise.

Hundreds of years later after the removal of David's tabernacle, Amos writes that a day is coming when God will restore the tabernacle of David and build it as it used to be. To understand what the Spirit of God is saying through the prophet Amos, let's first address what He is *not* saying.

The Holy Spirit is not telling us there will be a literal, physical restoration of the tabernacle of David. The ark of the covenant will not be placed in a tent again. Neither will we board a 747 jet and go to Jerusalem to worship.

When the woman at the well (John 4) asked where to worship, Jesus told her clearly that true worship was determined not by geographical location but by heart attitude and obedience to the Word of God. Praise and worship was not to be relegated to a certain place or area. It was to be expressed in spirit and in truth. It was to be expressed from the innermost part of man and done according to the Word of God.

The Spirit of God is revealing through Amos that a day is coming when the priestly and spiritual ministry of worship conducted in David's tabernacle will be restored. I believe that we are living in that day right now!

God Has a Purpose

God has a purpose for everything He does. He never does anything without a reason. By understanding His purpose, we can become part of His plan. The Bible tells us why God sent Jesus to earth. "For this purpose the Son of God was manifested, that He might destroy the works of the devil" (1 John 3:8, emphasis added). Likewise, God has a purpose for restoring the tabernacle of David.

3

When we tell our children to do something, they may respond with the question "Why?" We often answer, "Because I said so!" That alone is a good enough reason for them to do what we tell them. But at times it is a good idea to let them know why. If we tell them not to put their fingers in electrical outlets or not to play in the middle of the street, they should know the reason – that they could get killed if they do! Your children may thereby be persuaded that "to obey is better than sacrifice" (1 Sam. 15:22).

Now God is a loving heavenly Father and knows that man desires to have a purpose. He has placed that desire within us. Therefore, He gives us reasons for the restoration of the tabernacle of David involving praise and worship. After Amos declares that God is going to restore and rebuild the tabernacle of David, God's purpose for the restoration is revealed: "so that they may possess..." (Amos 9:12, NIV). Here we see God's prophetic purpose for the restoration of the ministry of praise and worship: possessing.

To understand what is being communicated we must first define the word possess. This is the Hebrew word *yaresh* which means to "occupy by driving out the previous tenants, to cast out, to consume, to destroy, to disinherit." God is restoring the tabernacle of David so that the church will have an instrument of warfare

4

to drive out, cast out, consume and destroy the works of darkness, disinherit the devil and occupy the earth. Hallelujah! Jesus was manifested for the same reason that praise and worship are being restored – to destroy the works of the devil.

An Example of Possessing

In 1992, America was engaged with the nation of Iraq in a military conflict known as the Gulf War and Operation Desert Storm. The primary reason for this war was that Iraq had illegally invaded and taken over the nation of Kuwait.

Although the United Nations Security Council issued resolutions to the nation of Iraq stating that Iraq had acted illegally and must withdraw its troops from Kuwait, Saddam Hussein, the leader of Iraq, chose to ignore the resolutions. That meant one thing: for the people of Kuwait to repossess their land, their enemy (the Iraqi army) would have to be driven out. In other words, war was inevitable because their enemy would not voluntarily get out of their country.

The offensive plan of Operation Desert Storm drove out the Iraqi army physically. To possess Kuwait, it took an offensive, physical, aggressive act of war. We were not there just to defend Israel, Saudi Arabia and the other surrounding countries. We were there to possess by driving out the previous tenants.

Our enemy, Satan, is even more lawless than Saddam Hussein. The devil will not voluntarily give you back what he has stolen from you. Jesus said, "The thief comes only to steal" (John 10:10). For the Israelites to possess Canaan, they had to go to war. To possess what is promised to you, you will have to enter into spiritual warfare. Remember, Canaan is an example of the blessings of God that have been promised and given to you. But just like the Israelites, you will have to go to war to take full possession and occupy your land.

The apostle Paul writes, "For the weapons of our warfare are not carnal, but mighty through God to the pulling down of strongholds" (2 Cor. 10:4). He also writes, "For we wrestle [war] not against flesh and blood, but against principalities" (Eph. 6:12). We must understand that the Bible teaches that we, the church, are to enter into spiritual warfare and fight with spiritual weapons.

Praise is one of the weapons God has given us. It is not a carnal weapon, but a spiritual weapon of war. God is restoring the tabernacle of David today. He is restoring the priestly ministry of praise, and we are to enter into it "so that [we] may possess." It is so that we, the church, may drive out our enemy, the devil, and receive our rightful inheritance.

CHAPTER TWO

OUT OF THE MOUTH OF BABES

*From the lips of children and infants
you have ordained praise, because of
your enemies, to silence the foe and
the avenger* (Ps. 8:2, NIV).

As stated earlier, God has a purpose for
everything He does. Thus far we have discovered God's purpose for restoring the tabernacle
of David: so we may have a weapon of warfare
to drive out the forces of darkness and take
possession of what God has given to us.

Have you ever wondered why God commands and desires our praise? Is it because He
has an ego problem? Is He insecure? Does He
need our praise? The answer to all these questions is emphatically no. God is not insecure,
even though we would consider someone who
needed continual praise to be insecure. God
does not need our praise. Scripture records
that there are creatures in heaven that do

nothing but worship Him day and night (Rev. 4:8).

Why then has God ordained our praise? Psalm 8:2 gives us the answer: "because of our enemies." Some people feel they have done the Lord a great service if they spend thirty minutes worshipping Him. The fact is we do not do Him a favor; we do ourselves a favor and the devil great damage. God has not ordained praise because He needs it, but because we need to praise Him.

Ezekiel refers to Lucifer as "the anointed cherub."

> *Thou hast been in Eden the garden of God; every precious stone was thy covering, the sardius, topaz, and the diamond, the beryl, the onyx, and the jasper, the sapphire, the emerald, and the carbuncle, and gold: the workmanship of thy tabrets and of thy pipes was prepared in thee in the day that thou was created. Thou art the anointed cherub that covereth; and I have set thee so* (Ezek. 28:13-14).

Lucifer was called to lead all of heaven in worship to the most high God. He was a "one-man band" with instruments built into his body. He was a masterpiece fashioned and formed for the purposes of God. But Lucifer fell because of pride.

*How art thou fallen from heaven, O
Lucifer, son of the morning! how art
thou cut down to the ground, which
didst weaken the nations! For thou
hast said in thine heart, I will ascend
into heaven, I will exalt my throne
above the stars of God: I will sit also
upon the mount of the congregation, in
the sides of the north: I will ascend
above the heights of the clouds; I will
be like the most high. Yet thou shalt
be brought down to hell, to the sides of
the pit* (Is. 14:12-15).

Because of a prideful heart, Satan fell
from heaven, lost his heavenly anointing, and
was cast to the earth. He had not rightly dis-
cerned the call, anointing, and gift God had
given to him. God had given him a glorious
ministry. This ministry was to bring all heaven
into a united symphony of praise unto the Lord.
His ministry was one that would cause him to
live in the presence of God before His throne
continually. He would have had the privilege of
being known as God's most beautiful creation.
But iniquity was found in him, and he lost it
all.

*By the multitude of thy merchandise
they have filled the midst of thee with
violence, and thou hast sinned: therefore
I will cast thee as profane out of the
mountain of God: and I will destroy
thee, O covering cherub, from the midst*

of the stones of fire. Thine heart was lifted up because of thy beauty, thou hast corrupted thy wisdom by reason of thy brightness. I will cast thee to the ground, I will lay thee before kings, that they may behold thee. Thou hast defiled thy sanctuaries by the multitude of thine iniquities, by the iniquity of thy traffic; therefore will I bring forth a fire from the midst of thee, it shall devour thee, and I will bring thee to ashes upon the earth in the sight of all them that behold thee (Ezek. 28:16-18).

The good news is that the devil's loss was our gain! I think God turned to the devil and said something like this, "I gave you a glorious ministry, yet you became consumed with yourself rather than Me. You disdained the ministry that I gave you, and because of this I revoke your heavenly anointing and heavenly position, and you will be cast down to the ground."

"As further punishment to you, I will take the ministry of praise and worship that you forsook and give it to a group of people on earth that shall be known as the church. Every time they enter into this ministry of worship, the ministry that you forsook, they will silence and paralyze you. They will take up the ministry of praise and worship and with it bind you, break you, bruise you and ultimately destroy your kingdom!"

The wonderful thing God did was to take what Satan was originally anointed to do and allow us, the body of Christ, to use it as a weapon of warfare to destroy his plans.

Psalm 8:2 says that God has ordained praise because of our enemy, to silence the avenger. The word "silence" is the Hebrew word *shabath* which means "to cause to fail, to repose, suffer to be lacking, to put down, take away."

As we praise the Lord, we cause the enemy to fail. As we lift our voices to God, we defeat the power of Satan that would bring us into bondage. As we enter into worship, we begin to take back what the enemy has stolen from us.

When you understand this, spiritual warfare is no longer drudgery. That's why Paul could say, "Fight the good fight of faith" (1 Tim. 6:12). It's a good fight when you know your enemy is fleeing in terror.

God desires to give us a new mentality regarding the devil and his works. He has been thought of as being the big, bad wolf, and we, the body of Christ, are the three little pigs. Our perception of spiritual warfare is as follows:

Knocking at the door, Big Bad Wolf says, "Little pig, little pig, let me in!"

11

"Not by the hair of my chinny chin chin. I resist you in Jesus name!" replies the little Christian pig.

"Then I'll huff and I'll puff and I'll blow your house down," says Big Bad Wolf.

And the little pig's house is blown down because it was built out of the wood, hay, and stubble of improper understanding. Being a good born-again, Spirit-filled, little pig, he runs crying to Pastor Pig, wanting him to pray for him.

This has been the church's mentality in the past concerning the devil, but now it's time to rewrite the story. I believe the present version would go something like this: Big Bad Wolf comes knocking at the door demanding to be let in. Now this little pig, realizing Big Bad Wolf has no right to be at his house, prepares his double-barreled weapon of warfare with a load of the high praises of God. He returns to the front door to greet Big Bad Wolf with his weapon in hand. As he unloads both barrels on Big Bad Wolf, he proclaims to the neighbors, "Wolf hunting season is now open!" The force of revelation-knowledge from the firing of the gun defeats the threat and secures his house.

I only use this story as an analogy to illuminate the change that must come to the mentality in the church. Instead of seeing the devil as a threat, I believe we need to see ourselves as a threat to his kingdom or as the object of his fear.

We are not running from our enemy; instead, we have him on the run. We are not in a defensive position waiting for him to attack. Rather, we take the offensive and assault his kingdom aggressively. We are God's commandoes who go in behind the lines rescuing those that are held captive. We use spiritual weapons of war to demolish his communications facilities and destroy his MO (method of operation).

Praise and worship play an important role in all of this because God has ordained our praise to silence him. Again, in Psalm 8:2, the psalmist declares that it is out of the mouth of babes that God has ordained praise.

Does that mean praise is reserved for children only? Not at all. Jesus said, "Unless you...become like little children you will never enter the kingdom of heaven" (Matt. 18:3, NIV). He said to "suffer little children...to come unto me: for of such is the kingdom of heaven" (Matt. 19:14). Jesus exhorted us to be like children. Likewise, the psalmist is saying in Psalm 8 that if we praise and worship the Lord like children, He has ordained that type of praise to silence and still the enemy.

When children praise the Lord, they are uninhibited. Their expressions of praise are as natural as breathing. I have three children, Joshua, Kayla and Micah. When they were toddlers and heard music, they would move, sway and dance to it. It was a natural response.

It should be just as natural to us as children of God to dance and celebrate before the Lord when we hear music and songs of praise. But sadly we have become religiously "brain-dirtied" over a process of time. The only solution is to wash our minds with the Word of God (see Eph. 5:26). We will then begin to worship in spirit and in truth as we behold what the Bible has to say about praise and worship.

It is time for the church to arise in this hour and praise the Lord with all its might. We must become uninhibited in our praise, even as children are. Then our weapon of warfare – praise – will be unleashed on the powers of darkness and result in their demise and destruction.

CHAPTER THREE

EXECUTING JUDGMENTS

*Let the high praises of God, be in
their mouth, and a twoedged sword in
their hand; to execute vengeance upon
the heathen, and punishments upon
the people; to bind their kings with
chains, and their nobles with fetters of
iron; to execute upon them the judgment written; this honor have all the
saints. Praise ye the Lord (Ps. 149:6-
9).*

This particular passage of Scripture has
always been one of my favorites. The part that
praise plays in spiritual warfare is evident as
you read it. With high praises and the Word of
God (a two-edged sword) we have the ability to
execute God's vengeance, inflict punishment,
bind kings, bind nobles and execute judgments.

In spiritual warfare, our enemy is not
people. As noted earlier, Paul said that "**we**

wrestle not against flesh and blood, but against principalities, against powers, against the rulers of the darkness of this world, against spiritual wickedness in high places" (Eph. 6:12, emphasis added). We must always keep in mind who our enemy is: the devil. Our problem is not people, but the spiritual forces that are motivating them. That realization will keep us focused on the mission God had given us to destroy the works of the devil.

Further, Paul said that "the weapons of our warfare are not carnal, but mighty through God to the pulling down of strong holds" (2 Cor. 10:9). You cannot fight a spiritual enemy with natural weapons. We must use spiritual weapons of war to combat our spiritual enemy. Praise is one of those weapons. It is a spiritual weapon of war that binds and breaks the powers of darkness.

As stated before, our praises can execute God's vengeance. God does take vengeance, for He said, "Vengeance is mine" (Rom. 12:19). God wants to settle the score in all matters and give just recompense to whom it is due. The primary target of that vengeance is the devil.

Next, in Psalm 149:8, we see that our praise will "bind kings with chains and nobles with fetters of iron." Let's first understand who the kings and nobles are that the psalmist is talking about. I believe them to be the principalities and rulers of darkness. They are the wicked demonic kings that have set up ruler-ship and dominion in geographical locations and in people's lives. The Bible says that our praise binds them with chains and fetters of iron. As we praise the Lord, we immobilize them. We cause them to desist and stop what-ever maneuvers, plans or strategies they are at-tempting to carry out.

The last thing that this passage reveals about our praise is that it "execute(s) the judg-ment written." The New International Version states it this way: "to carry out the sentence written against them."

To understand what is being said, visu-alize a court scene. There are many partici-pants in court: judge, jury, defendant, plaintiff, bailiff and witnesses, along with the lawyers who represent the accused and the accuser. All of them play an important role in the outcome of a trial. After the lawyers have presented their cases before the judge and jury, the jury will meet together for deliberation of the evi-dence. After deciding whether the accused is innocent or guilty, they will return with a ver-dict. The verdict will then be read out loud. If found guilty, the convicted criminal will have to stand before the judge for sentencing.

Now let's suppose that someone has just been tried for armed robbery. After hearing testimony and seeing evidence, the jury decides the defendant is guilty. He stands before the judge to be sentenced. The judge pronounces a judgment or sentence upon him, saying, "I sentence you to twenty years in the state penitentiary." It would be wonderful if that alone took care of the punishment, but it doesn't. The bailiff – a courtroom police official – handcuffs the convicted criminal, puts him in a police vehicle and takes him to the penitentiary where he is incarcerated and begins to serve his term.

This act by the bailiff is the execution of the judgment that is written. The judgment or sentence by itself will not do the job. Someone must see to it that the judgment is executed or carried out.

What if in that same courtroom there was no bailiff? Do you think the convicted criminal would voluntarily check himself into the penitentiary as someone would into a hotel? Could you envision him arriving at the front gate saying, "I have a reservation for the next twenty years?" No, without a bailiff, the convicted criminal is going to run out of that courtroom, never to be seen again.

Spiritually speaking, a judgment and a sentence have been pronounced on the devil. The Word of God declares that Satan and his works are beneath our feet (Rom. 16:20). It declares that all his power has been spoiled. But this is just the pronouncing of the sentence. That sentence, or judgment, must still be executed.

We (the church) are the bailiffs in God's great courtroom (the earth) where He sits as judge. Our praise binds the devil just as a police official handcuffs a criminal. Praise incarcerates him. The praises of God have divine power to execute the judgment decreed over the enemy.

The devil is a convicted criminal, and God has a warrant out for his arrest. What are we going to do about it? Let us as the church of God arise with praise in our mouths, as we execute His judgment upon the powers of hell.

At the end of Psalm 149 we read, "This honor have all the saints" (v.9). What honor is the psalmist talking about? It is the honor of executing God's judgment and vengeance on the powers of the air. Warfare praise is not a toilsome thing. It is an honor that God has bestowed upon you and me. It is done with joy in our hearts as we celebrate the victory of our Lord.

I once wondered why God didn't cast the devil into hell immediately after his rebellion. His punishment was rather to be confined to the earth to be punished by the church. We now have the honor of binding him. We have the honor of executing God's judgment and destroying Satan's kingdom.

Knowing this can change the way we view that which the devil attempts to throw across our paths. When confronted by the enemy, we have the privilege and honor of showing the devil who we are in Christ and the victory we possess. We then lift up our hands, raise our voices in song and dance before the Lord as we acknowledge Jesus as the mighty man of war who is mighty in battle through us!

CHAPTER FOUR

BEAT YOUR PLOWSHARES INTO SWORDS

Proclaim this among the nations:
Prepare for war! Rouse the warriors!
Let all the fighting men draw near and
attack. Beat your plowshares into
swords and your pruning hooks into
spears. Let the weakling say, "I am
strong!" (Joel 3:9-10, NIV).

Joel paints a good picture here of the army of the Lord in the last days. God is instructing us to prepare for war and rouse the warriors. Then He tells how: "Beat your plowshares into swords." There is an important revelation in this verse that the body of Christ needs to hear. Let's not miss it.

The prophet Hosea declares, "Judah shall plow" (10:11). The name *Judah* means "praise." Thus, the prophet is saying, "Praise shall plow." At some time you might have heard this statement in church: "Let's praise the Lord and prepare our hearts to receive the Word of God." I used to get a little upset about that phrase because it seemed to de-emphasize worship. But that is a very scriptural statement. As we praise the Lord, we plow and prepare our hearts to receive the incorruptible seed, the Word of God. Any farmer knows that before he plants seed he must first prepare the soil by plowing. Before we can plant the incorruptible seed of the Word of God, we must first plow the ground, our hearts, in which it is to be planted.

Praise and worship act as that plow. That's one of the reasons they come before the teaching and preaching of the Word rather than after it. Seed has a greater opportunity of bearing fruit when it's planted in plowed soil. Again, Judah (praise) shall plow.

Notice then what the prophet Joel says about your plow: "Beat your plow into a sword." I believe the Spirit of God is saying, "Make your praise a weapon of war." How do we do this? Revelation-knowledge is the hammer we use to beat our plows into swords, to make praise a weapon of war.

One principle governing spiritual experiences in the kingdom of God is: **revelation is needed for appropriation through faith.** Hearing the Word brought revelation for appropriating our salvation by faith. Hearing the Word also brought revelation for appropriating the infilling of the Holy Spirit. Likewise, to be able to use praise as a weapon in spiritual warfare we must first have a revelation that God has ordained our praise for such a purpose.

There is a difference between celebration and having a revelation of your celebration. Praise and celebration without a revelation of its power have little effect in the realm of the spirit.

Let me give you an example. We could take a drunk man off the street and bring him into church. This man could say the sinner's prayer simply by repeating what he was told. But, if there was not first a revelation of the Lordship of Jesus and the fact that God raised Jesus from the dead, that man would go away just as unsaved as he was before he said the sinner's prayer. Why? It is because he said words without understanding and revelation.

Unfortunately, much of the church is like that. We come to church and praise the Lord with no understanding and revelation of the power God has placed in our praise. Consequently, nothing happens.

The solution is to receive a revelation of what the Bible has to say about praise and worship, particularly in its application as a weapon of spiritual warfare. Then, when we come together to praise and worship the Lord, there will be a release of God's power which will begin to affect the spirit realm.

> *I will gather all nations, and will bring them down into the valley of Jehoshaphat, and will plead with them there for my people and for my heritage Israel (Joel 3:2).*

This verse has great significance to us as the people of the Lord. Jehoshaphat's enemies were defeated by the praises of God in the valley of Jehoshaphat. (A later chapter will deal with this in more depth.) This account is found in 2 Chronicles 20. When faced with insurmountable odds, Jehoshaphat appointed singers and musicians to go out at the head of the army to praise the Lord. As they praised the Lord, God brought confusion in the camp of the enemy, and they rose up and destroyed one another. So we could say that the valley of Jehoshaphat is the place where praise ascends.

This sheds new light on this Scripture verse. Where does God enter into judgment? It is in the valley of Jehoshaphat, the place where praise ascends. Where are God's judgments executed? It is in the valley of Jehoshaphat, the place where praise ascends. God's judgments are executed on our enemy, the devil, when praise ascends, just as in the day of Jehoshaphat.

The word of God declares that all the things that were written in the Old Testament were written for our example. The story of Jehoshaphat was not penned by the Spirit of God so that we would have another good Bible story to tell our children. Rather, it was written so we could be "followers of them who through faith and patience inherit the promises" (Heb. 6:12). This was written so that we can see with our physical eyes what our praise does in the spirit realm.

Another verse in Joel 3 reiterates the same thing:

> *Let the nations be roused; let them advance into the Valley of Jehoshaphat, for there I will sit to judge all the nations on every side* (Joel 3:12, NIV).

I believe the Spirit is calling the church in this hour to become a radical, militant people who are warriors in the Spirit. Don't use the old excuse, "Well you know, that's just not my personality." Being a warrior has nothing to do with your personality. It has to do with the family you belong to. If you are born of God you are a warrior because His seed is in you and He is a warrior. Hallelujah! You have been drafted into the army of the Lord. Don't go AWOL. Get in the fight as God leads us into victorious battle.

Beat your plowshares into swords and your pruning hooks into spears. Let the weakling say, "I am strong!" (Joel 3:10, NIV).

We sing several songs that contain this phrase: "Let the weak say, 'I am strong.'" The location of this verse is very interesting. In the context of Scripture, it refers to people who are getting themselves ready to go to war. It is an exhortation for those who feel too weak to go out and fight to rouse themselves by declaring that they are strong! This was a Scripture passage given for warriors.

As a matter of fact, the word translated "strong" is the Hebrew word *gibbor.* It means "warrior" or "tyrant." The verse actually says, "Let the weak say, 'I am a warrior.'" The Spirit of God is prophetically telling the body of Christ to declare, "We are warriors."

I like that word "tyrant." Tyrants strip all rights and privileges from their subjects. We need to be tyrants in the spirit! We shouldn't give the devil an inch. Rather, we need to strip all rights and privileges from him that he has stolen from us. It is time for us to take our stand in the spirit.

To some people, speech like this may sound as if I am a mean person. But my natural personality is not that of a fighter. I was in only a few fights in all of my school years. They were very short – the guy hit me, and I hit the ground. The fight was over. But what I am saying is that we must become violent when it comes to fighting devils. Jesus said, "The violent take it by force" (Matt. 11:12).

I believe the Spirit of God is crying for the church to arise in strength and maturity. It is time for us to run to the battle with our weapons of war without looking back. We must be like Gideon's army. The Bible says they were "faint, yet pursuing" (Judg. 8:4). When you begin to feel faint, take a dose of the Word of God. "Let the weak say, 'I am strong.'" Rouse yourself and take up your sword and wield it against your enemy. Let your praise become a weapon of war as you lift your voice to Him!

CHAPTER FIVE

MIGHTY MAN OF WAR

The Lord is a warrior; the Lord is his name.
Pharaoh's chariots and his army
he has hurled into the sea.
(Ex. 15:3-4, NIV)

The Lord will march out like a mighty man,
like a warrior he will stir up His zeal;
with a shout he will raise the battle cry
and will triumph over his enemies.
(Is. 42:13, NIV)

I saw heaven standing open
and there before me was a white horse,
whose rider is called Faithful and True.
With justice he judges and makes war.
(Rev. 19:11, NIV)

The Bible reveals that part of God's character is that of a warrior. Both the Old and New Testaments testify of this. As members of the body of Christ and to engage successfully in spiritual war, we need to have this revelation of God's character.

Paul told the Ephesians to be "imitators of God" (Eph. 5:1, NIV). And to be imitators of God, we must have a revelation of His whole character. Not only is He a God of love, peace and joy, but He is also a warrior. Paul said, "Behold therefore the goodness and severity of God" (Rom. 11:22). Paul is saying we can see the whole character of God by looking at the whole counsel of the Word of God.

If we emphasize one aspect of the character of God, then we get a distorted picture of who God is. For the past couple of decades a great deal of teaching has come forth on the goodness and love of God. I thank God for all we have learned. But, it seems as if we have had little teaching on some of the other attributes of His character. One of those is the attribute of warrior.

Why is it important to teach this attribute? First, what you reach in God will be in direct proportion to your revelation of Him. Someone who does not have a revelation of Jesus as Savior cannot receive Him as their Savior. Someone who does not have a revelation of Jesus as healer, *Jehovah Rapha*, will not get healed. Likewise, without a revelation of Jesus as warrior, the Lord of Hosts, we will not be able to wage successful, spiritual warfare. God moves on our behalf according to our faith and knowledge of Him.

The second reason for teaching on this attribute of God's character is so we will know in what atmosphere the Lord manifests Himself as a warrior. This is where praise and worship enter the picture. As we study the following Scripture passages, we will see that Jesus arises as a mighty man of war in the midst of praise and worship. Something about praise stirs the heart of God. As we praise, He rises up with a zeal and vengeance against our enemies.

> *Sing to the Lord a new song, his praise from the ends of the earth, you who go down to the sea, and all that is in it, you islands, and all who live in them. Let the desert and its towns raise their voices; let the settlements where Kedar lives rejoice. Let the people of Sela sing for joy; let them shout from the mountaintops. Let them give glory to the Lord and proclaim His praise in the islands* (Is. 42:10-12, NIV).

Here we see an exhortation for people to praise the Lord. By the Spirit of God, Isaiah instructs them to raise their voices, rejoice, sing a new song, shout, sing for joy, give glory to God and proclaim His praise. The next verse tells us what happens when people express their praise to the Lord:

> *The Lord will march out like a mighty*
> *man, like a warrior he will stir up his*
> *zeal; with a shout he will raise the*
> *battle cry and will triumph over his*
> *enemies* (Is. 42:13, NIV).

What happens when we praise the Lord? The Lord marches out against our enemies. As we lift our voices to the Lord with shouts of joy, His zeal is stirred. As we glorify God with heart, soul and strength (spirit, soul and body), the battle cry arises, and He triumphs over our enemies.

The original Hebrew language contained no punctuation marks. All punctuation has been placed there by the translators. Without changing the words, **I would like to take the liberty of changing a few punctuation marks.** I believe this will enable us to see this verse in a different light.

> *The Lord will march out like a mighty*
> *man, like a warrior. He will stir up his*
> *zeal with a SHOUT! He will raise the*
> *battle cry and will triumph over his en-*
> *emies.*

What is revealed to us is that the zeal within the heart of God is stirred with shouting of praises. We could even read it like this: *The Lord will march out like a mighty man, like a warrior. His zeal will be stirred with shouts of praise.*

31

To substantiate this as a scriptural principle, here are some other Scripture passages that say essentially the same thing:

> O clap your hands, all ye people; shout unto God with the voice of triumph. God is gone up [ascended] with a shout (Ps. 47:1,5).

> "God has ascended amid shouts of joy" (Ps. 47:5, NIV).

> Every stroke the Lord lays on them [the enemy] with his punishing rod will be to the music of tambourines and harps, as He fights them in battle with the blows of his arm (Is. 30:32, NIV).

The emphasis is on the connection between our praise and God's battle with our enemy. As we rejoice and shout, God arises in our midst and scatters our enemies.

> "May God arise, may his enemies be scattered; may his foes flee before him" (Ps. 68:1, NIV).

When God arises, His enemies are always scattered. The devil is no match for almighty God and His church. The key to successful spiritual warfare is God arising.

So how does He arise? Psalm 47:5 says He arises amid shouts of joy. Isaiah 42:13 declares that His zeal is stirred with a shout, and in the midst of that He raises the battle cry, triumphing over His (and our) enemies. Isaiah 30:32 says that every stroke the Lord lays on our enemy is done "to the music of tambourines and harps" as He fights them with the blows of His arm. That's the reason the psalmist could say: "His right hand, and his holy arm, hath gotten him the victory" (Ps. 98:1).

The psalmist had a revelation that God would fight on our behalf as we praised His name. He had a revelation of the Lord as the mighty man of war. He knew that the Lord would march out on our behalf if we would shout His praise in faith.

The psalmist David was a man after God's own heart (1 Sam. 13:14, NIV). I used to think it was because David was a lover of God. After further study of David's life, I do not believe that was the only reason he was referred to as a man after God's own heart.

David was a man who had a reputation in the kingdom of Israel. Saul asked his servant to find someone to play the harp before him. Let's observe what the servant ascribed to David (1 Sam. 16:18): He knows how to play the harp. He is brave. He is a warrior. He speaks well. He is fine-looking. The Lord is with him.

Knowing how to play a harp and speak well and be fine-looking would not make you a man after God's own heart. But notice what the testimony concerning David also alleged. He was brave, he was a warrior, and the Lord was with him.

Nobody else in Israel was jumping at the chance to face Goliath, except David, the warrior – the man after God's own heart. No one else in Israel was willing to risk his life to fight a lion and a bear for a sheep, except David, the warrior – the man after God's own heart. When Saul told David he could marry his daughter if he brought him one hundred Philistine foreskins (1 Sam. 18:25), David slew enough Philistines to double the requirement: David **the warrior – the man after God's own heart.**

Yes, David was a worshipper and a lover of God, but he was equally a warrior, a man of war. David knew his God and did everything within his power to be like Him.

David was a warrior, but there was one who was an even greater warrior than David. His name was Jesus. He warred against sin, sickness, religious traditions of men, hypocrisy and many other things. In Matthew 21 we can see one of the greatest demonstrations of this aspect of God's character: Jesus' triumphal entry into Jerusalem on the back of a donkey.

"Say to the Daughter of Zion,
'See, your king comes to you,

> gentle and riding on a donkey,
> on a colt, the foal of a donkey...'"

> A very large crowd spread their cloaks
> on the road, while others cut branches
> from the trees and spread them on the
> road. The crowds that went ahead of
> him and those that followed shouted,

> "Hosanna to the Son of David!"
> "Blessed is he who comes in the
> Name of the Lord!"
> "Hosanna in the highest!"

> When Jesus entered Jerusalem, the
> whole city was stirred and asked, "Who
> is this?" The crowds answered, "This
> is Jesus, the prophet from Nazareth in
> Galilee" (Matt. 21:5, 8-11, NIV).

Let's examine what was happening. Meek
and gentle Jesus was riding into Jerusalem on a
donkey. On His way to the temple, a large
crowd began to have an outdoor praise celebration in honor of Him. Many were taking off
their cloaks and laying them in the road for
Jesus to pass over. Others were cutting down
branches from trees and laying them in the
road. All of them were shouting praises so
loudly that the "whole city was stirred."

When Jesus arrived at the temple, something happened:

Jesus entered the temple area and drove out all who were buying and selling there. He overturned the tables of the money changers and the benches of those selling doves. "It is written," he said to them, "'My house will be called a house of prayer,' but you are making it a 'den of robbers'" (Matt. 21: 12-13, NIV).

The blind and the lame came to him at the temple, and he healed them. But when the chief priests and the teachers of the law saw the wonderful things he did and the children shouting in the temple area, "Hosanna to the Son of David," they were indignant. "Do you hear what these children are saying?" they asked him. "Yes," replied Jesus, "have you never read, "'From the lips of children and infants you have ordained praise'?" (Matt. 21:14-16, NIV).

I want you to see what motivated Jesus to go into the temple and drive the money changers out. I do not believe it was merely the activities of the money changers, because Jesus had seen them before at the temple. It was not the selling of the doves, for this had been going on for years, and Jesus had never done anything about it.

What caused Jesus to arise with righteous indignation in a violent assault against these men? **It was the shouts of praise that were coming from the people.**

When Jesus first entered Jerusalem, He was meek and gentle. But, as He rode through town toward the temple, there was a metamorphosis. As the shouts of praise were lifted to Him, His zeal was stirred just as Isaiah 42:13 declared. At no other time in the history of His walk on earth had there been such an open demonstration of praise, worship and celebration in honor of Him. The Lord was getting ready to "march out like a mighty man" as He heard the praises of the people.

Upon arriving at the temple, having been stirred by the shouts of praise, He made a whip out of some cords (His punishing rod) and proceeded to drive out the money changers. He then began to overturn the tables of the dove salesmen.'

In chapter one of this book, we saw that God is restoring the tabernacle of David for a purpose. That purpose is to possess. We learned that the word "possess" means *to drive out the previous tenants.* "Jesus entered the temple area and *drove out* all who were buying and selling there" (Matt. 21:12, NIV). In the midst of a praise celebration Jesus drove out the previous tenants (the money changers) and then

37

declared, "My house will be called a house of prayer." In essence He was saying, "This is My house, and you can't have it!" He possessed what was rightfully His.

Verses 15 and 16 of Matthew 21 reveal an interesting event. The chief priests and teachers of the Law, the religious leaders of the day, were indignant when they heard the children shouting praises to the Lord. Demonstrative praise and worship always upset religious spirits. Demons of pride hate shouting and dancing because it is not "dignified."

Those in leadership in the body of Christ today must not mimic the response from the religious leaders of Jesus' day. They did not get upset with Jesus about the miracles He did that day or the fact that He had just caused a big ruckus in the temple. They got upset because people were **praising demonstratively**! They tried to get Jesus to tell the people to stop. But Jesus told them, "If these should hold their peace, the stones would immediately cry out" (Luke 19:40).

The people who were throwing their cloaks in the road and cutting down branches were never accused by Jesus of being "in the flesh." There is no place in the Bible where it says to take off your coat and throw it in the road in praise to the Lord. Neither is there any place where it says to cut down the branches and throw them in the road in praise to the

Lord. Yet the people did that, and Jesus never rebuked them. As a matter of fact, you cannot find anywhere in the Bible where Jesus ever rebuked people for praising and worshipping God. He encouraged and defended the ones who did.

A lesson can be learned from this. Anything you can do to glorify God, as long as it does not go contrary to Scripture, do it! If you can glorify God with a laser light show, then do it! If God can be glorified through dance presentations, then do them! He is not opposed to our using creativity in our worship expression.

The only people who discouraged and condemned demonstrative worship were religious leaders. As these teachers of the Law heard the children praising Jesus, they asked Him: "Do you hear what these children are saying?" (Matt. 21:16, NIV).

Jesus began His reply by saying, "Yes, have you never read...?" Let me point out here that it would do many people good to read what the Bible teaches about worship. Jesus went on to say "From the lips of children and infants you have ordained praise." Of all the passages on praise that Jesus could have quoted, He chose Psalm 8:2.

From the lips of children and infants
you have ordained praise because of

your enemies, to silence the foe and the avenger (NIV).

Note how the verse concludes: "Because of your enemies, to silence the foe and the avenger." Jesus was not only defending the activity of these children, but He was also explaining everything that had just happened in the temple area. He was saying, "This is why I came into the temple and drove out the money changers. This is why I overturned the tables of the dove salesmen. God has ordained praise like that from these children because it causes Me to rise up against My enemies (the money changers) and put them to silence." Hallelujah

We have heard it said, "If Jesus healed then, He is still healing today. If Jesus delivered then, He is still delivering today." These statements are true. But, let me propose this to you: if in the midst of praise and worship Jesus arose as a man of war then, He is still arising today. He is the same yesterday, today and forever. Our God is a warrior!

CHAPTER SIX

THE ROAR OF THE LION OF JUDAH

But one of the elders said to me, "Do not weep. Behold, the Lion of the tribe of Judah, the Root of David, has prevailed to open the scroll and to loose its seven seals" (Rev. 5:5, NKJV).

In this passage of Scripture, it is clearly articulated that Jesus is the Lion of Judah. We know that Jesus came from the tribe of Judah. The lion was actually the emblem of this tribe in Israel. It was the lion that was supposed to be embroidered on its ensigns. Today, the lion is still the emblem for the city of Jerusalem. It is on both the flag and the coat of arms for the city.

What is interesting about this verse is the fact that the Holy Spirit took opportunity to use this terminology when referring to Jesus. He could have just as easily said "Jesus has prevailed" or possibly, "The Lamb of God has prevailed." However, the Spirit of the Lord did not say that. He said, "The lion of the tribe of Judah...has prevailed." There must be something of value meant for us if the Holy Spirit wanted this to be written.

The lion is referred to many times as the king of the jungle. He is considered to be noble, stately, and kingly. Historically, the lion has meant different things to different peoples and cultures. The lion was used to allegorically depict the Messiah through the character of Aslan in the book entitled, **The Lion, the Witch, and the Wardrobe.**

So, the question we are presented with concerns the attribute of the Lord that the Holy Spirit desired to reveal when He referred to Jesus as the Lion of the tribe of Judah. Was it merely that He was kingly and noble? Although that may be a part of it, I don't believe that is its entirety. I believe there is much more. This was not a descriptive name that was being used arbitrarily.

We understand that the name *Judah* means *praise*. So when the Bible says the "Lion of Judah," we could also say: the Lion of Praise. Jesus is the Lion of Praise. He manifests Himself as a lion in the midst of praise. It is in the place of praise and worship that He reveals Himself as the Lion of Judah.

42

The one thing that is associated with lions more than anything else is their ROAR. When a lion roars, it does several different things. One of the primary things that it does is **paralyze its prey**. The sound of the roar produces fear and terror in the heart of its victim to the point that it cannot move. To the prey, it is a sound that evokes the emotion of panic and alarm because of the king of the jungle. Before the lion pounces on its find, it will roar to announce it. With this in mind, let's consider this verse found in Amos 3:4, "Will a lion roar in the forest, when he has no prey? Will a young lion cry out of his den, if he has caught nothing?" (NKJV).

The spiritual reality is that Satan, our enemy, is overcome with spiritual paralysis as the Lion of Judah begins to roar in the midst of our praise and worship. The enemy realizes that he has been discovered and the lion announces with His roar, "You are my prey." This roar that is released in the midst of our praise causes the enemy to go into a state of panic. He is paralyzed so that he cannot function or operate. The Lion of Judah has prevailed and the enemy is defeated. Hallelujah!

As believers, we must realize that there is no truce that has been drawn between us and Satan. He is the enemy of our soul and he hates every Christian. In this spiritual warfare that we are in, it is either kill or be killed. There is no demilitarized zone. The good news is that Jesus is the Lion of Judah. He is the king of the jungle (the ruler of the earth). It is in the midst of our praise that He will roar and our enemy will be devoured.

Sometimes, people have exaggerated the roar of the devil and minimized the roar of the Lord. We must remember that the devil is a counterfeiter. The only reason that he goes about as a roaring lion (1 Peter 3:8) is because he counterfeits. The devil has never been and never will be an originator. He only perverts that which is real and genuine.

I believe that we need to focus more on the roar of the Lion of Judah than the roar of the poser. The roar of the Lord will consume the lies of hell. The word of the Lord will trump any kind of sound that the devil could even hope to make. Jesus is all-powerful and there is none like Him.

We must understand that the roar of the Lord is greater. The Apostle John said, "Greater is He that is in you than he that is in the world." The roar of the Lion of Judah in you is greater than the roar of the enemy. The roar of the Lord released within His people through praise will annihilate the work of the enemy.

God has created us to respond to His roar because it is His voice in the earth. We have been designed as new creatures in Christ Jesus to hear and respond to His roar. But, there are many believers today who react to the roar of the enemy with fear rather than respond to the roar of the Lord with faith. Again, this is a perversion of that which God created. The reality is that we will respond to a roar. The question becomes which one we are going to hear? We should choose to hear the roar of the Lion of Judah so that faith will arise and victory will be secured.

We see biblically that the roar of the lion is used as an analogy of **God fighting for His people.**

> *For thus the LORD has spoken to me: "As a lion roars, And a young lion over his prey ..., So the LORD of hosts will come down To fight for Mount Zion and for its hill* (Is. 31:4, NKJV).

We have had much teaching in the body of Christ concerning the present day ministry of Jesus. We have heard that He is our mediator and intercessor. However, we have heard little about Him warring and fighting for His people.

We see in this passage of Scripture that as the Lion of Judah roars, He will fight for His people. The roar is an indication that the fight is on. When the Lion of Judah roars, it indicates that there is war in the spirit realm and the enemy is being routed. Again, it is in the midst of praise and worship that He roars.

Another principle that we see in the Bible is that the roar of the lion is compared to God speaking and the prophetic ministry.

Surely the Lord GOD does nothing, Unless He reveals His secret to His ser- vants the prophets. A lion has roared! Who will not fear? The Lord GOD has spoken! Who can but prophesy? (Amos 3:7-8, NKJV).

Notice the comparison that is being made between the lion roaring and God speaking. This is another thing that begins to take place in the midst of our praise. There is a release of the prophetic ministry. God begins to be stirred within His people and the voice of the Lord is manifested.

Although we will share more detail later on in this subject, it is the voice of the Lord that will shatter the enemy. The roar of the Lion of Judah shatters the enemy. It is the sound of His voice, the voice of the Lord, which edifies believers and simultaneously destroys the enemy. So while we are being built up and encouraged, the enemy is being torn down and destroyed. It is the roar of the Lion that causes this to be manifested in our lives.

The roar of God is food for the believer and poison for the enemy. It is that which the enemy despises hearing. Yet, for believers it is a sound that declares triumph and victory.

We must understand that lions do not roar to announce defeat. They roar to announce the demise of their prey. When God roars, He is announcing the defeat of the enemy and His triumph. He is indicating to all who have ears to hear that He is King and Lord and that every foe is trampled. It is in the midst of praise that this roar is heard.

In relationship to the prophetic ministry being released in praise, let's look at another passage of Scripture.

> *But now bring me a musician. "Then it happened, when the musician played, that the hand of the LORD came upon him. And he said, "Thus says the LORD: 'Make this valley full of ditches.' For thus says the LORD: 'You shall not see wind, nor shall you see rain; yet that valley shall be filled with water, so that you, your cattle, and your animals may drink.' And this is a simple matter in the sight of the LORD; He will also deliver the Moabites into your hand (2 Ki 3:15-18, NKJV).*

It is very interesting that as Elisha needed to hear from God, he asked for a musician to begin to play and worship. It was understood that music was designed to be an expression of holy celebration and worship. This was not a rock concert where vulgarities and booze were flowing. This was a time of worship.

So, as the musician began to worship, God began to speak. We could say that as praise and worship began to be expressed, the Lion of Judah began to roar. His voice was heard. It was a voice of victory and triumph. As we read verse eighteen, we see that God announces the defeat of the Moabites. God was roaring through the prophet to announce His victory and the defeat of the enemy.

This is what happens in the midst of praise today. The Lion of Judah arises to roar. His roar announces the defeat of the enemy and the victory that we have in Christ Jesus. As this roar is heard, the enemy is frightened and terrified! This is exactly what happened to the Moabites and will happen to your enemy, too!

Let's look at another passage of Scripture concerning the roar of the Lord.

> They shall walk after the LORD. He will roar like a lion. When He roars, Then His sons shall come trembling from the west. (Hosea 11:10, NKJV)

We see here that the roar of the Lion of Judah is **a cry for the sons and daughters of the Lord to return.** It is a sound that bids the prodigals to come home. It is a sound that is released in the spirit that causes hearts to come back to God.

At the beginning of 2010, I called for fourteen days of prayer that was to begin on January 4th at our church. We opened the church up in the mornings for people in the congregation to join in intercessory prayer. We also had special prayer meetings on Thursday evenings and Sunday afternoons before our evening service. On the 14th day which was January 17th, there was a spiritual breakthrough that took place that resulted in a spiritual birthing of a fresh move of God in our church.

It was during the evening service that I began to hear a roar in the spirit realm. I did not realize at that time the full impact that this would have on our congregation. I understand now that it was a roar that was announcing a fresh move of God that would cause prodigals to come back into the kingdom of God. Not only did I hear it in that service, but there were two other services where there was a distinct spiritual roar that was heard.

In the six weeks following that service, there were more people who received salvation and more prodigals who returned to the Lord than in the entire previous year. Many who were not serving the Lord experienced the conviction of the Holy Spirit come upon them while at home. They rededicated their lives to the Lord and began coming to church. There have been children of those within our church who have come to their senses and returned to the Lord after years of being backsliders.

Supernatural demonstrations of the miraculous power of God resulting in medically documented healings of incurable diseases have been taking place. Cancer and incurable sexually transmitted diseases have been healed. Broken relationships have been restored. Broken families have been put back together. God has done awesome things.

What is interesting about all of these happenings is the fact that the roar of God was released before and during these occurrences. We see in Hosea 11:10 how that "when He roars, then His sons shall come." It is the roar of the Lion of Judah that breaks through the clutter of the sound of this world and brings conviction into the heart of the sinner. It is His roar that breaks the chains of the enemy and brings the release of His supernatural power.

Today, we need the roar of the lion of Judah to be restored to the church. It is that roar which will bring freedom and deliverance.

Many years ago, I wrote a song entitled "Roar O Lion of Judah." I'll close this chapter with the words of that song:

> Roar, O Lion of Judah, Roar
> Rise, O Mighty Man of War
> Roar, O Lion of Judah, Roar
> Rise, O Mighty Man of War
>
> Rise up within Your people
> And make a sound of war
> Declaring that Your enemies are slain
> For none can stand before you
> And the power of Your Name
> Forever Your kingdom will reign

CHAPTER SEVEN

IN THE PRESENCE OF THE LORD OF HOSTS

"But thou art holy,
O thou that inhabits the praises of Israel."
(Ps. 22:3)

The Lord is my strength and song, and
he is become my salvation: he is my
God, and I will prepare him an habita-
tion; my father's God, and I will exalt
him. The Lord is a man of war: the
Lord is his name (Ex. 15:2-3).

I will praise thee, O Lord, with my
whole heart; I will show forth all thy
marvelous works. I will be glad and re-
joice in thee: I will sing praise to thy
name, O thou most High. When mine
enemies are turned back, they shall fall
and perish at thy presence (Ps. 9:1-3).

Most Christians have probably heard at
one time or another that God inhabits the

praises of His people. Before a worship service begins, a pastor will often exhort the congregation: "Let us come this morning and allow the presence of God to be manifested as we praise Him. The Word of God declares that God inhabits the praises of His people. Allow the Lord to inhabit your praise as you lift your voice in song to Him."

But lack of knowledge or religious "mindsets" have hindered us from understanding the nature and work of God who inhabits our praise.

For most Christians, the only revelation of God's character is that of a loving, merciful Savior. Thank God we have that revelation. If it were not for the love and grace of God, we would all be lost and without hope. But God's character is more than just love and grace, as wonderful as those attributes are.

We learned in the previous chapter that our God is a man of war. He is a warrior. The Bible also refers to God as the Lord of hosts. The word "hosts" is the Hebrew word *tsaba*. This word means "a mass of persons organized for war." So when the Bible refers to the Lord as the Lord of hosts, it is referring to the Lord of armies or the Lord of people organized for war. As a matter of fact the Bible refers to God as the Lord of hosts in 244 places. This is five times more than any other descriptive or redemptive name ascribed to Him.

In the New Testament God is referred to twice as *Lord of Sabaoth*. The word "sabaoth" is the transliteration of the Hebrew word *tsaba* meaning "armies." **Strong's Concordance** defines this Greek word as "a military epithet of God." God wants us to know that He is Lord of a fighting and warring people.

After the children of Israel crossed the Red Sea, God displayed His mighty power in the destruction of the Egyptian army.

And the Lord said unto Moses, Stretch out thine hand over the sea, that the waters may come again upon the Egyptians, upon their chariots, and upon their horsemen. And Moses stretched forth his hand over the sea, and the sea returned to his strength when the morning appeared; and the Egyptians fled against it; and the Lord overthrew the Egyptians in the midst of the sea. And the waters returned, and covered the chariots, and the horsemen, and all the host of Pharaoh that came into the sea after them...and Israel saw the Egyptians dead upon the sea shore (Ex. 14:26-28,30).

God spoke to Moses to stretch out his hand over the sea so that the Egyptians would be drowned. The waters collapsed on the Egyptians and they were totally annihilated. The Israelites saw dead bodies scattered along the seashore. At this sight, Moses told them to strike up the band.

> Then sang Moses and the children of
> Israel this song unto the Lord, and
> spake saying, I will sing unto the Lord
> for he hath triumphed gloriously: the
> horse and the rider hath he [God]
> thrown into the sea (Ex. 15:1).

On seeing the enemy destroyed, Moses decided it was time to celebrate. They began to sing a song of praise to the Lord, most likely in an antiphonal manner. (An antiphonal song is carried out in responsive, alternating parts. Usually the worship leader sings a short phrase, and the congregation then echoes it.) They rejoiced and danced for the mighty victory that had just been wrought. In fact, they praised the Lord for killing the Egyptian army.

Visualize this for a moment: The Israelites had just crossed the Red Sea, and now there were dead Egyptians bodies lying on the shore. As the Israelites are singing, Miriam the prophetess takes a tambourine and begins to lead all the women in dance there on the seashore. They were rejoicing in song because the judgment of God had been executed upon their enemies.

Many of us have sung "The Horse and the Rider" as a nice, joyful, praise song that is fun to sing. But we are actually praising the Lord for destroying – killing – the Egyptian army.

As Moses and the children of Israel were celebrating, they sang, "I will prepare him an habitation" (Ex. 15:2). How do we prepare a habitation for God? Psalm 22:3 says that God inhabits the praises of His people. We prepare a habitation for God with our praise. Our praise creates a place where God can dwell and manifest His presence.

The Bible tells us that God inhabits or is enthroned in three places: in heaven, in our hearts as believers and in our praise.

We want to concentrate on the third – God being enthroned in our praise. Knowing that God inhabits our praises, we then proceed to find out the character and nature of Him for whom we are preparing a habitation. We have already established that the Lord is a warrior and that He is the Lord of hosts. Our God is militant. Our praise prepares a habitation for the mighty warrior, the Lord of hosts. Moses had a revelation of this. Immediately after saying, "I will prepare him an habitation," he said, "the Lord is a man of war: the Lord is his name" (Ex. 15:3).

The manifest presence of God is the tangible (sensed or felt) manifestation of God's character and nature. At one time or another, all of us have probably sensed His presence in our lives.

Since God's character and nature are multifaceted, so is the presence of God. When you sense the peace of God in a worship service, you are sensing a manifestation of *Jehovah-Shalom*. If you sense a healing anointing, God is manifesting Himself as *Jehovah-Rapha*, the Lord our Healer. These more familiar manifestations of the presence of God may have been the extent of our revelation of God's character and nature. God responds to us according to our faith.

Jesus said, "According to your faith be it unto you" (Matt. 9.29). We have had limited faith to receive the presence of God except as love, peace, joy, healing and deliverance. God's presence will be manifested according to our revelation of His character and nature.

I do not believe the Lord desires to stay in the box we have built for him through limited revelation of who He is. I believe He is bringing revelation of His character and nature that will allow Him to flow freely as He desires to manifest His presence with might and great power. The Lord wants to manifest His presence as the mighty man of war, the Lion of Judah and Lord Sabaoth. He desires to reveal Himself to us as the Lord of hosts who is mighty in battle.

God has a purpose for His manifest presence. **First** of all, God desires to minister to us with His presence. The Bible says, "In thy presence is fullness of joy" (Ps. 16:11). We are to be a joyful people.

Second, God desires to minister through us with His presence. When God manifests His presence as *Jehovah-Rapha*, we should pray for others to receive their healing. I equate this to the story of the angel who troubled the waters at the pool of Bethesda. Whoever stepped in first was healed (John 5:4). When God's presence is manifested in a healing anointing it is easier to get people healed. At that time, as colaborers with God, we need to step out and minister to one another.

Finally, God wants to destroy our enemies with His presence. God's presence is manifested for the purpose of spiritual warfare. Psalm 68:2 says, "Let the wicked perish at the presence of God." David said in Psalm 9:3, "When mine enemies are turned back, they shall fall and perish at thy presence."

As Moses declared, we prepare a habitation for the Lord who is a man of war. If we prepare a habitation for the Lord who is a man of war, then God desires to show Himself to us in that manner. A man of war fights. Our praise prepares a habitation for the Lord to manifest Himself as the mighty man of war and rise up and fight against our enemies.

We are co-laborers with God, working together with the Lord. When we sense the presence of Lord Sabaoth, the Lord of hosts, the Lord is actually sounding the battle cry for His army to follow Him into battle.

We may sense a "spirit of warfare." This is when God's Spirit prompts us to enter with our weapons of praise into spiritual warfare against the spirits of darkness. **This is the presence of God.**

As you read the story of David meeting Goliath, you can see that David had a revelation of the Lord of hosts. After the giant threatened him, he declared prophetically the fate of Goliath.

> *Thou comest to me with a sword, and with a spear, and with a shield: but I come to thee in the name of the Lord of hosts, the God of the armies of Israel, whom thou hast defied* (1 Sam. 17:45).

David was saying, "It is not my sling and stone that will kill you, but it is my God, the Lord of hosts, who will serve as my weapon." Goliath came against David with natural weapons, but David was armed with the revelation that the God he served was the Lord of hosts. It was David's trust in that revelation that caused his sling and stone to be empowered by God.

Likewise, that revelation of the God who inhabits our praises will give power to our praises. We will be able to say with David, "[My enemies] shall fall and perish at thy presence" (Ps. 9:3).

God's presence is not manifested to give us a spiritually euphoric experience. We must know that the One who inhabits our praises is almighty God, the mighty warrior, the Lord of hosts. Not only is there fullness of joy in His presence, but there is also complete victory, as the Lord Sabaoth leads us into battle, and His enemies perish at His presence.

CHAPTER EIGHT

THE POWER OF THE SHOUT

Clap your hands, all you nations; shout to God with cries of joy...God has ascended amid shouts of joy, the Lord amid the sounding of trumpets (Ps. 47:1,5, NIV)

Let God arise, let his enemies be scattered: let them also that hate him flee before him. As smoke is driven away, so drive them away: as wax melteth before the fire, so let the wicked perish at the presence of God (Ps. 68:1-2).

The Lord will march out like a mighty man, like a warrior he will stir up his zeal; with a shout he will raise the battle cry and will triumph over his enemies (Is. 42:13, NIV).

There are many different ways the Bible tells us to express our praise to the Lord.

Shouting is one of those ways. Exactly why God desires us to shout, I do not know. But, nonetheless, He has told us to shout to Him. He has also laid out in the Word of God spiritual principles for the shout.

To the natural mind, shouting to God seems silly. After all, God is not hard of hearing and does not need us to speak a little louder. But the Word of God reveals that the shout releases something in and through us. God established the shout of praise for our benefit.

The word "shout" is the Hebrew word *ruwa*. It means "to split the ears with sound; to mar especially by breaking." God has put power in shouting. When we shout, we split the devil's ears with praise. We mar and break up his kingdom. The fortresses the enemy had built begin to crumble and fall as we shout praise to the Lord.

In chapter five, we examined the account of Jesus' triumphal entry into Jerusalem. In the midst of this praise Jesus arrived at the temple and drove out all the money changers and dove salesmen.

In the account of the triumphal entry we see a demonstration of a spiritual principle. Psalm 47:5 declares God arises amid shouting. In the King James Version we read, "God is gone up with a shout." The word "gone" is the

Hebrew word *alah*. One of the definitions for this word is "stir up." So we could read that verse like this: *God is stirred up against our enemies when we shout His praise.*

We see this spiritual principle demonstrated in the triumphal entry of Jesus and the cleansing of the temple. Let's look at it from a little different angle. Psalm 68:1 says "Let God arise, let His enemies be scattered." How do we let God arise? We have already established that God arises or is stirred up with shouting. The Hebrew word translated *arise* in this passage is defined as "to rise, rouse up, stir up."

We see that when God arises or is stirred up, His enemies are scattered. The word *scattered* means "to dash in pieces or break." Now, let us put it all together and see what's actually being said:

God is stirred up against our enemies with shouts of praise. As He is stirred up, or arises, His enemies are dashed into pieces, and their kingdoms are broken and destroyed.

This brings us back to the original definition of *shout*, which is "to mar by breaking." As mentioned earlier, the accounts and stories written in both Old and New Testaments were written for our example (1 Cor. 10:11) and to demonstrate spiritual principles. Let's look at some that demonstrate the principle of the shout. One of the most familiar accounts is that of Joshua at Jericho, found in chapter 5 and 6 of Joshua.

Now when Joshua was near Jericho, he looked up and saw a man standing in front of him with a drawn sword in his hand. Joshua went up to him and asked, "Are you for us or for our enemies?"

"Neither," he replied, "but as commander of the army of the Lord I have now come." Then Joshua fell facedown to the ground in reverence, and asked him, "What message does my Lord have for his servant?" The commander of the Lord's army replied, "Take off your sandals, for the place where you are standing is holy." And Joshua did so (Josh. 5:13-15, NIV).

Then the Lord said to Joshua, "See, I have delivered Jericho into your hands, along with its king and its fighting men. March around the city once with all the armed men. Do this for six days. Have seven priests carry trumpets of rams' horns in front of the ark. On the seventh day, march around the city seven times, with the priests blowing the trumpets. When you hear them sound a long blast on the trum-

pets, have all the people give a loud shout; then the wall of the city will collapse and the people will go up, every man straight in" (Josh. 6:2-5, NIV).

The story unfolds as the commander of the army of the Lord approaches Joshua. Interestingly enough, Joshua does not recognize who it is. He has never seen the Lord like this. The Lord is standing with a drawn sword. Joshua has known the Lord as deliverer, provider and sustainer but not as warrior. The Lord appears to Joshua to give him a fresh revelation of who He is so that he can carry out the mission of God.

He then receives battle instructions from the Lord – a divine strategy. The Lord instructs Joshua to march around the city of Jericho one time each day for six consecutive days. On the seventh day, they are to march around the city seven times. Then the priests are to sound a long blast on the trumpets, and the people are to "give a loud shout." At this, the walls will fall.

Joshua then instructs the people and proceeds to carry out the battle plan.

On the seventh day, they got up at daybreak and marched around the city seven times in the same manner, ex-

*cept that on that day they circled the
city seven times. The seventh time
around, when the priests sounded the
trumpet blast, Joshua commanded the
people, "Shout! For the Lord has given
you the city!"... When the trumpets
sounded, the people shouted, and at
the sound of the trumpet, when the
people gave a loud shout, the wall collapsed; so every man charged straight
in, and they took the city* (Josh. 6:15-
16,20, NIV).

As all the people gave a loud shout, the
walls collapsed. Again, we have to ask why this
story is in the Bible. Of course, one reason is
because it was a historical event that actually
happened. But Paul declared that these things
were written for our example. So what are the
principles and truths God wants to reveal to us
in this story?

One is simply the blessing of obedience.
But a spiritual principle governed even the
practice of obedience. I believe the principle
was that of the power of the shout!

Another truth is that of the necessity of a
divine strategy. But then why did God use the
strategy of offering up a shout? Could this be
used again, or was it just an isolated incident?
It was to be an example for us to follow.

God was demonstrating the mighty weapon of the shout through the Israelites. God arises amid shouts of praise, and His enemies are scattered. As Joshua and the Israelites shouted, their enemies' defense was destroyed. When we shout unto God with a voice of triumph, the defense of our enemies is destroyed, and we are able to go in and spoil his goods. We can go up and possess what rightfully belongs to the church. Hallelujah!

The account of Gideon and the Midianites demonstrates another great victory involving shouting.

Dividing the three hundred men into three companies, he placed trumpets and empty jars in the hands of all of them, with torches inside. "Watch me," he told them. "Follow my lead. When I get to the edge of he camp, do exactly as I do. When I and all who are with me blow our trumpets, then from all around the camp blow yours and shout, 'For the Lord and for Gideon.'"

Gideon and the hundred men with him reached the edge of the camp at the beginning of the middle watch, just after they had changed the guard. They blew their trumpets and broke the jars that were in their hands. The three companies blew the trumpets and smashed

*the jars. Grasping the torches in their
left hands and holding in their right
hands the trumpets they were to blow,
they **shouted**, "A sword for the Lord
and Gideon!" While each man held his
position around the camp, all the
Midianites ran, crying out as they fled*
(Judg. 7:16-21, NIV, emphasis added).

Once again we see how shouting is used
in warfare. As the Midianites heard the trumpets and the shouting, they ran in terror. The
Bible goes on to tell us that the men of the
Midianite army turned on each other and began
to kill one another. Confusion was brought into
the camp of the enemy through the joyful
sound. As the Midianites heard the shout they
scattered.

In the book of 1 Kings, we find another
interesting account concerning two of David's
sons. One was named Adonijah; the other was
named Solomon. As King David lay dying, a
question arose as to who would be king in
David's place. Adonijah decided that he would
take advantage of the situation and usurp the
throne to be king. He gathered men around him
who would agree to his plot, and he proclaimed
himself as king.

Nathan the prophet, upon hearing of
Adonijah's uprising, told Bathsheba, David's
wife and the mother of Solomon. He instructed
her to make David aware of Adonijah's rebel-

lion. She was to remind David of his promise to make Solomon king. When David heard of Adonijah's behavior, he instructed Nathan the prophet and Zadok the priest to get Solomon and anoint him king over Israel. Then he said, "Blow the trumpet and shout, 'Long live King Solomon!'"

> *So Zadok the priest, Nathan the prophet, Benaiah son of Jehoiada, the Kerethites and the Pelethites went down and put Solomon on King David's mule and escorted him to Gihon. Zadok the priest took the horn of oil from the sacred tent and anointed Solomon. Then they sounded the trumpet and all the people **shouted**, "Long live King Solomon!" And all the people went up after him, playing flutes and rejoicing greatly, so that the ground shook with sound* (1Ki. 1:38-40, NIV, emphasis added).

These passages picture an inaugural celebration. All the people shouted and rejoiced until the "ground shook with the sound." Can you imagine this? The intensity of sound in the Super Dome with a capacity crowd may not have been as loud as it was on that day.

Meanwhile, Adonijah was feasting with all his friends, probably talking about the changes he would make now that he was king. While they were feasting across town, they heard the noise. Jonathan, son of Abiathar the priest, ran in to tell Adonijah and his guests the reason for the celebration. After the announcement was made, "...all Adonijah's guests rose in alarm and dispersed" (1 Ki. 1:49, NIV).

As a result of the people's rejoicing and shouting "Long live King Solomon," Adonijah's men were gripped with fear and scattered. Adonijah was so afraid that he took hold of the horns of the altar and would not let go until he got word that Solomon would not kill him.

As the people shouted, the usurpers were scattered. They rose in alarm and dispersed. When Satan hears the shouts of God's people proclaiming Jesus as king, he and his demonic powers flee in alarm. We terrorize the devil with shouts.

The home-field advantage in sports competition also demonstrates the principle of the shout. Playing at home gives a team an advantage because more people will cheer – shout – for the home team. These shouts can demoralize the visiting team and sap its enthusiasm, zeal and energy.

These shouts cause the home team to play more aggressively, with a greater degree of confidence. You may ask how this relates to Christians. In one sense, we are in a competition. It's Jesus and the church against Satan and his demonic powers.

We have the home-field advantage. The Bible says that the "earth is the Lord's, and the fullness thereof; the world, and they that dwell therein" (Ps. 24:1). The Lord owns the stadium in which the church competes. The devil is the visiting team. Having been kicked out of heaven, the devil is visiting earth on his way to hell.

Church members and heavenly beings fill the stadium. As they cheer and shout, someone many times greater than the best National Football League quarterback enters the playing field. Our quarterback, Jesus, calls the plays as He instructs the church in what to do. His plays are prophetic insight, revelation, activation and demonstration. The devil does not have a chance as the people in the stadium shout praises and cheer for Jesus.

I use this analogy only to help you understand what power God has invested in the shout. We are not trying to compare Jesus with famous earthly quarterbacks. There is no comparison. These analogies deepen our understanding of the principles God has ordained in His Word.

A fellow minister related a story of an exercise he participated in while in the U.S. Air

Force. The exercise involved hand-to-hand combat with pugil sticks. During the exercise his opponent struck him with a forceful blow to the abdomen, knocking the breath out of him. He then fought back, landing several good blows.

At that point, his comrades began to shout and cheer at a deafening level. The shouts stimulated the rush of extra adrenaline and strength, resulting in the defeat of his opponent.

Once again a shout stirred up zeal. This is a spiritual principle that God has put into operation, and it applies even in natural things.

Several years ago I was leading worship in a church that was holding a prophetic conference. Little did I know that God was going to teach me firsthand the power of the shout.

The conference began on a Tuesday evening and ended on Sunday evening. I sensed one of the most oppressive atmospheres I had ever been in as we began the conference. I was tired from a day of travel and thought perhaps that was why I felt as I did; it would be different in the morning.

But the next morning a heavy, oppressive spirit still hung over the church. Worship never took off. No one was praising the Lord, and no spiritual gifts were being manifested.

Forty-five minutes of worship seem like an eternity when a sense of freedom and God's presence are not evident. At the end of the service, I analyzed the situation. Maybe it's just that it's a morning service, and people are not fully awake yet, I thought. Tonight we'll have a real breakthrough.

The Wednesday evening service came, but no breakthrough came with it. By this time I was becoming very concerned. This is going to be a really long conference, I thought, if things do not change fast. I sought the Lord about how to break through this oppressive spirit.

As I led worship for the fourth time in the conference, the same pattern repeated itself. In the middle of worship, the Spirit of God spoke to me and said, "Have everyone shout, and tell them not to stop until you tell them to." So I told the congregation what the Lord had spoken to me. We shouted for twenty minutes. About ten minutes into the shouting, something broke open in the spirit realm, and the oppressive spirit left.

In the midst of the shouting, the Lord gave me a vision of the heavenly host coming forth in pursuit of a demonic army in retreat. God was routing the enemy as we were shouting unto the Lord with the voice of triumph. God arose, and His enemies were scattered.

From that point on, there was freedom in the services. The worship was exciting as people entered into praise during each service. The gifts of the Spirit were manifested as people were healed, delivered and set free. But the release came as a result of the twenty minutes of shouting we did on Thursday morning.

My friend, we need to have an understanding that there is power in the shout of victory. As we lift our voices, God will arise and our enemies will be scattered!

CHAPTER NINE

JEHOSHAPHAT'S REVELATION

In 2 Chronicles chapter twenty, we read the account of what I call Jehoshaphat's dilemma. Three different armies had gathered together against Judah. Jehoshaphat, king of Judah, was faced with insurmountable odds. He was a "dead duck" unless God moved on his behalf.

"Alarmed, Jehoshaphat resolved to inquire of the Lord" (2 Chron. 20:3, NIV). He decided it was time to "seek the Lord while he may be found" (Is. 55:6, NIV).

As the people of Judah sought the Lord, the Spirit of the Lord came upon a temple musician named Jahaziel who prophesied the word of the Lord.

And he said, Hearken ye, all Judah, and ye inhabitants of Jerusalem, and thou king Jehoshaphat, Thus saith the

*Lord unto you, Be not afraid nor dis-
mayed by reason of this great multitude; for the battle is not yours, but
God's. Tomorrow go ye down against
them: behold, they come up by the cliff
of Ziz; and ye shall find them at the
end of the brook, before the wilderness
of Jeruel. Ye shall not need to fight in
this battle: set yourselves, stand ye
still, and see the salvation of the Lord
with you, O Judah and Jerusalem: fear
not, nor be dismayed; tomorrow go out
against them: for the Lord will be with
you.*

*And Jehoshaphat bowed his head with
his face to the ground: and all Judah
and the inhabitants of Jerusalem fell
before the Lord, worshipping the Lord*
(2 Chron. 20:15-18).

Jahaziel prophesies battle instructions to
the nation of Judah. He prophesies that they
will not need to fight because God has a different plan of warfare for them. He also prophesies that they are to march out against the
enemy on the next day.

As Jehoshaphat receives the prophetic
strategy from the Lord on the following day, he
gives the people a little pep talk.

*Early in the morning they left for the
Desert of Tekoa. As they set out,*

Jehoshaphat stood and said, "Listen to me, Judah and people of Jerusalem! Have faith in the Lord your God and you will be upheld; have faith in his prophets and you will be successful" (2 Chron. 20:20, NIV).

Then Jehoshaphat does one of the most unorthodox things ever done by a commander-in-chief of an army.

After consulting the people, Jehoshaphat appointed men to sing to the Lord and to praise him for the splendor of his holiness as they went out at the head of the army, saying: "Give thanks to the Lord, for his love endures forever" (2 Chron. 20:21, NIV).

Can you imagine this? He puts the band and the singers at the front of the army. Either God was going to do something great, or there would be no more music in the nation of Judah!

People volunteer to be on our church worship team. I wonder how many volunteers Jehoshaphat had that day. Their lives, in fact, depended on their worship. If it didn't prove to be successful, there would be no second chance. What faith in the prophecy from Jahaziel these men had.

Then they proceeded to march out against their enemy with the praises of God in their mouths.

As they began to sing and praise, the Lord set ambushes against the men of Ammon and Moab and Mount Seir who were invading Judah, and they were defeated. The men of Ammon and Moab rose up against the men from Mount Seir to destroy and annihilate them. After they finished slaughtering the men from Seir, they helped to destroy one another. When the men of Judah came to the place that overlooks the desert and looked toward the vast army, they saw only dead bodies lying on the ground; no one had escaped. So Jehoshaphat and his men went to carry off their plunder, and they found among them a great amount of equipment and clothing and also articles of value – more than they could take away. There was so much plunder that it took three days to collect it (2 Chron. 20:22-25, NIV).

A mighty victory was wrought as God's people sang praises unto the Lord. Singing praises unto the Lord causes confusion to come into the camp of the enemy. According to Bill Hamon, founder and president of Christian International Network of Prophetic Ministries, prophetic praise is God's jamming device to confuse the demonic spirit communication channels, thereby causing their destruction.[1] Jehoshaphat had a revelation of the power of praise.

It is interesting that they praised the Lord for his mercy and love. To be truthful, I could never understand why they would sing about the mercy of God. I asked the Lord about this, and he showed me Jehoshaphat's revelation.

Jehoshaphat's revelation of mercy was different from ours in the church today. We see mercy in the light of the cross and our redemption. Jesus had not yet come to the earth when Jehoshaphat lived. Therefore, his revelation of mercy was different from ours. The song the nation of Judah sang as they went out against their enemy gives us some insight into his revelation.

Psalm 136

O give thanks unto the Lord; for he is good: for his mercy endureth forever. O give thanks unto the God of gods: for his mercy endureth forever. O give thanks to the Lord of lords: for his mercy endureth forever.

To him who alone doeth great wonders: for his mercy endureth forever.

79

To him that by wisdom made the heavens: for his mercy endureth forever. To him that stretched out the earth above the waters: for his mercy endureth forever. To him that made great lights: for his mercy endureth forever: the sun to rule by day: for his mercy endureth forever: the moon and stars to rule by night: for his mercy endureth forever.

To him that smote Egypt in their firstborn: for his mercy endureth forever; and brought out Israel from among them: for his mercy endureth forever: with a strong hand, and with a stretched out arm: for his mercy endureth forever.

To him who divided the Red sea into parts: for his mercy endureth forever: and made Israel to pass through the midst of it: for his mercy endureth forever: but overthrew Pharaoh and his host in the Red sea: for his mercy endureth forever. To him which led his people through the wilderness: for his mercy endureth forever.

To him which smote great kings: for his mercy endureth forever: and slew famous kings: for his mercy endureth forever: Sihon king of the Amorites:

for his mercy endureth forever: and Og the king of Bashan: for his mercy endureth forever: and gave their land for an heritage: for his mercy endureth forever: even a heritage unto Israel his servant: for his mercy endureth forever.

Who remembered us in our low estate: for his mercy endureth forever: and hath redeemed us from our enemies: for his mercy endureth forever. Who giveth food to all flesh: for his mercy endureth forever. O give thanks unto the God of heaven: for his mercy endureth forever (KJV).

Sung in responsive, alternating parts, this antiphonal song praises God for His love and mercy. Interestingly enough, over one-fourth of the song praises God for destroying the enemies of the people. Verses 10, 15 and 17-20 praise God directly for destroying their past enemies. Verses 11-14 and 24 praise God for His deliverance which resulted or culminated in the destruction of their enemies. Their revelation of God's mercy was that He would destroy their enemies. Their understanding of mercy was that their enemies did not have a chance.

The psalmist David had this same revelation and understanding of mercy when he wrote: "And of thy mercy cut off mine enemies, and destroy all them that afflict my soul: for I am thy servant" (Ps. 143:12).

David knew that God's mercy in action would be the destruction of all his enemies. Jehoshaphat realized God's mercy was militant.

Let me give you a natural example of mercy and love. A family has a swing set in their backyard on which the children play. If a mean dog were to come into the yard while the children were playing and attack them, the parents would not try to reason with the dog. Like all loving parents, they would run outside and yell at that dog! They might even have something in their hand to "execute judgment" upon that animal. Loving parents would do whatever necessary to eradicate the dog in the situation.

The actions against that animal are the result of parents showing love and mercy to their children. Parents get angry when they see someone or something hurting their children because they love them. It would be unmerciful and unloving if parents did not act in this manner.

Jesus said, "If ye then being evil, know how to give good gifts to your children, how much more shall your Father which is in heaven..." (Matt. 7:11). If we would destroy an animal that attacks our children, how much more will our heavenly Father war against the enemies or our souls?

Much of our understanding of mercy is not wrong; it is simply incomplete. I thank God for the cross and the blood of Jesus. But the revelation that Jehoshaphat and the children of Judah had was different from ours. We need to add Jehoshaphat's understanding of mercy and love to our own. Then, when we sing about the mercy of God, we will see the same results they experienced. It is the understanding and revelation we possess that allow God's power to be released as we sing. There is no power in singing without biblical understanding and Holy Ghost illumination of what is being sung.

The Bible records another account of a mighty victory that was won as a result of singing praises to the Lord.

> *And when they had laid many stripes upon them, they cast them into prison, charging the jailer to keep them safely: who, having received such a charge, thrust them into the inner prison, and made their feet fast in the stocks. And at midnight Paul and Silas prayed, and sang praises to God: and the prisoners heard them. And suddenly there was a great earthquake, so that the foundations of the prison were shaken: and immediately all the doors were opened, and everyone's bands were loosed* (Acts 16:23-26).

As Paul and Silas praised the Lord, two noteworthy events occurred. **First**, the foundations of the prison were shaken. This has great spiritual significance. The devil desires to put people in the prison of darkness, despair, oppression, sickness and sin. After Paul and Silas sang praises, an earthquake shook the foundations of the prison. When we sing, the very foundations of the kingdom of darkness are shaken.

Second, after the foundations were shaken, the prison doors flew open, and everyone's bands were loosed. In the midst of Paul and Silas's singing of praises, people were set free. God's power is also manifested when we come together and sing to Him.

Many years ago, I was leading worship at a Christian International Conference. During one of the services, a man's deaf ear popped open as we sang the second song. No one had laid hands on him or prayed for him. Thank God that in the midst of singing and rejoicing his "bands were loosed."

In January 1992, I was conducting a Prophetic Warfare Praise seminar in Columbia, South Carolina. We had dedicated the last night of the conference to waging war in the heavenlies with our praise. We had a tremendous breakthrough that night as we sang warfare songs. Many people gave their lives to Jesus as their "prison doors flew open" and their "bands were loosed."

> *And he hath put a new song in my mouth, even praise unto our God: many shall see it, and fear, and shall trust in the Lord* (Ps. 40:3).

As the people heard the praises to God, they put their trust in Him. The spirits that had blinded them to the gospel were pushed back as praise allowed their hearts to be wooed by the Holy Spirit.

Looking once again in 2 Chronicles 20 at the story of Jehoshaphat, we see two statements by Jahaziel that we still hear in churches today. One is found in verse fifteen: "The battle is not yours, but God's." Some say it this way, "The battle belongs to the Lord." The other is found in verse seventeen: "Stand ye still, and see the salvation of the Lord." Many think these verses mean to do nothing. That is not correct. Immediately after Jahaziel prophesied that the battle was the Lord's, he said in verse sixteen, "Tomorrow go ye down against them."

Also, after he told them to stand still, he said in verse seventeen, "Tomorrow go out against them." The Spirit of God was saying to the nation of Judah that they were not going to have to fight with natural weapons of war. This battle was not going to be won by the sword, but by a different kind of warfare.

Likewise, we must realize there is a fight to be fought, but not with natural weapons. God has given us weapons of praise that have power against principalities and the devil. As we go forth singing the praises of God, our enemy is turned back in confusion.

If Jehoshaphat and the nation of Judah had not marched against their enemies singing praises unto the Lord, there would have been no victory.

As one minister says, "God is a fair checkers player. You move, and then He moves."

Unless we take up our weapons of praise, God cannot arise on our behalf and destroy our enemies. Let us go forth and sing the praises of our Lord as he brings confusion to the camp of the enemy, resulting in great victory.

CHAPTER TEN

PRAISE HIM WITH UNDERSTANDING

*Oh, clap your hands, all you peoples!
Shout to God with the voice of triumph! For the LORD Most High is
awesome; He is a great King over all
the earth. He will subdue the peoples
under us, And the nations under our
feet. He will choose our inheritance
for us, The excellence of Jacob whom
He loves. Selah. God has gone up with
a shout, The LORD with the sound of a
trumpet. Sing praises to God, sing
praises! Sing praises to our King, sing
praises! For God is the King of all the
earth; Sing praises with understanding*
(Psalm 47:1-7, NKJV).

In the last verse of this passage of
Scripture, the Psalmist gives a prophetic directive that is often missed by many believers
today. That command is to "sing praises with
understanding." There are many today who

have adopted a contemporary form of praise
and worship into their churches and daily lives.
Unfortunately, if we have no understanding of
that which we are singing, or the character and
nature of the one we are praising, or the power
that God has invested in praise and worship,
our songs will become empty and powerless.
This Scripture gives us the key to seeing the
power and presence of God released in the
midst of our praise. That is praising Him with
understanding.

I believe that we could even say that the
Psalmist's intent was to articulate, in verses
one through six, the understandings that we
should have when we praise and worship the
Lord. The reason that this is so important is
because we do nothing more than make noise if
we don't have clear biblical understandings of
praise established within our hearts. We become like parrots that mimic that which they
hear, yet have no comprehension. God has a
higher level that we can operate within. This is
achieved by worshipping with revelation knowledge. The result is powerful praise released and
God's glory revealed.

SEVEN PRINCIPLES FROM PSALM 47

As we examine Psalm 47, there are seven
specific understandings that are clearly stated.
I want to share these with you so that your
praise and worship will become effective. I

refer to this as Seven Principles for Effective Praise.

The **first** principle is this: *GOD LIKES IT LOUD.* Notice that the Psalmist said "Shout unto God with the voice of triumph." I think we all have a clear understanding that there is nothing quiet about a shout. As a matter of fact, it's not a soft or mellow sound. It is loud, boisterous, and intense. One of the first things that believers need to realize is that it is good to get loud in your praise. Praise is designed by definition to be loud. Praise was never designed by the Father God to be soft and mellow.

When we define the word "shout" and the word "triumph," we can see clearly what the Bible commands all of us to do. The word "shout" is translated from the Hebrew word *rua* which means to split the ears with sound. The word "triumph" is translated from the Hebrew word *rinnah* which means a creaking or shrill sound. Also, the phrase "with the voice of" literally means a thundering voice or yell.

We see that God is giving to His people some clear instruction as to how He wants to be praised. In the opening verse of Psalm 47, God gives a directive to clap your hands and shout triumphantly. He actually adds "all you peoples." He left no one out! When God says "all," He means ALL. He didn't say for extroverts only. Nor did He say if you felt like it or if it was within the makeup of your personality.

I think it's very interesting today how people can go to a football game and watch a man carry a bag of wind (football) over a line drawn on a piece of real estate (goal line) and everyone in the stadium will go nuts. The officials will award that team six points. Although this will not change anyone's life in a major way, the people in the stadium will clap their hands and shout with the voice of triumph. Think about it.

On the other hand, we have people who have been redeemed by the blood of Jesus, delivered from the powers of darkness and hell, filled with His Holy Spirit and now have the power of God living on the inside of them who will not even lift their voice to say, "Hallelujah" in the midst of a gathering of believers. Yet, at a sporting event, they become the loudest people in the stadium. In the words of the Apostle James, "My brethren, these things ought not to be."

It is not wrong to shout at sporting events. It's just more important that you shout in church! It's not wrong to clap your hands when your team does well on the playing field. It's just more important that you clap your hands to the One who has redeemed you! It's not wrong to get excited about your favorite team winning a championship. It's just more important that you rejoice in the fact that we are now victors through Christ Jesus!

And the twenty-four elders and the four living creatures fell down and worshiped God who sat on the throne, saying, "Amen! Alleluia!" Then a voice came from the throne, saying, "Praise our God, all you His servants and those who fear Him, both small and great!" And I heard, as it were, the voice of a great multitude, as the sound of many waters and as the sound of mighty thunderings, saying, "Alleluia! For the Lord God Omnipotent reigns! (Rev. 19:4-6, NKJV).

Looking at a picture of heaven as we read Revelation nineteen, we can see that heaven is a loud place. The praise in heaven sounds like "mighty thunderings." To the surprise of many, they will find out that heaven is not a quiet place. It is filled with activity and filled with praise. It reverberates throughout the heavens as the saints who have gone on before, and the angels join together to give glory and honor to the Lord Most High.

If you ask the average Christian what they will do when they get to heaven, they will reply, "Praise the Lord." Yet, it's amazing how many of them have difficulty lasting through thirty minutes of worship during a church service. They are correct that they are going to worship God throughout eternity, but they also need to realize they should start while they are here on earth. They also need to realize that praise in heaven is loud. Therefore, praise on earth should be conducted in the same manner. Why? Because God likes it that way!

The Bible tells us to enter into the throne room with boldness, not fear or timidity. We don't sneak into the back door of heaven, crawling on our hands and knees with a sense of unworthiness. We come boldly with rejoicing and celebration in the reality that we are God's children; we have been redeemed by the blood of Jesus; and the devil is under our feet!

The primary Hebrew word that is translated praise is the word *halal*. This is where we derive our word "Hallelujah." This word means to be clamorously foolish. The word *clamorously* refers to a loud or deafening noise. The bottom line is this: praise involves the making of a loud and rowdy noise. Praise is not soft. Praise is not mellow. Praise is boisterous! Praise is loud!

Psalm 149:5 says that the saints are to "sing aloud on their beds." I don't believe that the Psalmist is literally telling us to go lie down on our beds and start singing loudly. But, there is a truth that is contained in this Scripture that will help bring further validity to the truth that God likes it loud.

The words "sing aloud" are actually translated from the Hebrew word *ranan* which means to emit a stridulous sound. The word "bed" is translated from the Hebrew word *mishkab* which by euphemism refers to carnal intercourse. Now, obviously the Psalmist is not talking literally in this passage of Scripture. In the context of this Scripture, he is talking about praise and worship. So, when he, by the Spirit of the Lord, uses this word *mishkab* which is translated "bed," he is talking about the spiritual exchange or intercourse that is to take place as we praise and worship the Lord.

The Lord is actually saying that as we have relationship with Him through praise, we should not be quiet or timid. Don't be afraid to get loud when you express your thanks and praise. God is saying that He likes it loud!

The **second** principle for effective praise is that *WE PRAISE FROM A POSITION OF VICTORY!* We do not praise to get victory. We praise from a place of victory. We are seated with Christ in heavenly places. Just as all things are under His feet, they are under our feet too!

The Scripture said to shout with the voice of triumph. The voice of triumph is the sound of one that has won already. The voice of triumph is the sound of victory. The voice of triumph is the sound that faith produces as it boldly declares, "I am more than a conqueror."

Many believers today have an improper perception of spiritual warfare. Spiritual warfare is not the enemy beating up on you while you stand there with no defense. Spiritual warfare is that which we do in taking up our weapons of warfare to advance the kingdom of God. It is the aggressive stance that we take as believers in Christ Jesus where we take the authority that we have been given and forcefully execute it within the earth. Although the enemy may oppose us with his evil tactics, we still arise in faith with the high praises of God on our lips, a shout of praise, and the sword of the Spirit that will cause us to prevail in every situation. This is spiritual warfare.

We must understand that we do not praise to get victory; we praise from a platform of victory. The Apostle Paul said that we are more than conquerors. He also said thanks to God who always causes us to triumph. Victory is not something that we will have one day; it is that which we possess now. It is this understanding that causes our praise to have power in the realm of the spirit.

The reality is that you already have all the victory that you will ever have. You don't need more victory because Jesus already gave His accomplished victory to you. We need that which we already possess to come into a place of full manifestation. Praise is one of the spiritual weapons that God has given to us that will enable this to take place within our lives. Your praise has the power to produce the visible manifestation of that which you already have. Victory will be realized as you go forward with the high praises of God on your lips and the sword of the Spirit in your hand!

The **third** principle for effective praise is the understanding that *GOD IS WORTHY OF OUR PRAISE BECAUSE HE IS AWESOME.* In verse two of Psalm 47 it declares, "For the Lord Most High is awesome." The word "awesome" literally means to be feared and reverenced. One thing that we need in the church today is a revival of the holy, reverential fear of God. It seems as though somewhere in the midst of teaching on grace and love, many have lost sight that He is God to be feared. Yes, He is Father, but He is first of all God.

The very first verse of the Bible reveals Him as God. I personally believe that a Christian must first have an understanding that He is God before they can receive Him properly as Father. The word that is used for God is the Hebrew word *Elohiym.* It refers to the Supreme Ruler and Magistrate. Effective praise will embody a revelation that He is God, the Supreme Ruler of all the earth. In other words; GOD RULES!

Unfortunately, some believers have developed a "Santa Claus" Jesus mentality. They believe that God is there only to make them feel good and give them a high self esteem. God would never rebuke or discipline them or allow them to go through any consequence produced by disobedience. He is just there to give out toys and candy to anyone who is saved regardless of their behavior or poor decisions. My friend, this is just not true. Although He loves us more than we can imagine or comprehend, it is His love that also brings correction and discipline.

I grew up in a home where I knew that my father loved me. He worked daily in order to provide for our family. He verbally communicated that he loved me. My parents were constantly involved in that which I participated. However, I realized that I better obey him or else I would receive the consequence of disobedience. I feared and reverenced my father. I knew that he loved me and I loved him, but I still had a healthy fear that made me walk right. I knew that in our family, daddy was the supreme ruler.

Much of the sin that is rampant in the church today is because people have lost sight that the Lord Most High is AWESOME – to be feared and reverenced. We need this understanding to return to the people of God. When people realize this, they stop sinning. Then, as the prophet Malachi declared, the offering of Judah will be pleasant unto the Lord. Praise that is offered up out of unclean vessels loses its power. Keeping sin out of your life and walking uprightly before the Lord is a key to having powerful praise that will bind the forces of hell. This is achieved when we realize that He is awesome.

The fact that God is worthy of our praise is almost something that could go unsaid since for most Christians this is not a foreign concept. We have numerous songs that state He is worthy. There are numerous Scriptures that state He is worthy. The only problem is that many don't understand what worthy actually means.

The root word of worthy is "worth." *Worth* refers to value that is placed upon something or someone. The way that we express our thanks and praise to the Lord says something of the value that we place upon the Lord. It expresses the worth of what He has done and is doing within our lives. Half-hearted and disconnected worship says that God has little value within our lives. Judging by the way that some praise and worship the Lord, one would question as to whether the Lord had any value within their lives.

If we are going to say with our mouths that He is worthy, then we should express that in a wholehearted manner that is fitting for the Lord Most High who is awesome. If we believe that He is awesome, then we should give Him praise in an awesome manner. If He is the Most High God, then we should give Him some high praise. If He is God, then we should lift up His name in a godly manner.

After all He's done for you and me, praise is the least that we can give to Him. The fact that Jesus came and gave His life to redeem me from the hold of the enemy is reason enough for us to dance, rejoice, shout and sing. We should not need some sort of prodding to get us going in worship. This should be that which naturally flows out of our hearts. I encourage you today to begin to praise Him because He, the Most High God, is worthy and He is awesome!

The **fourth** principle for effective praise is the understanding that *GOD RULES IN THE MIDST OF OUR PRAISE.* The Psalmist said that "He is a great king over all the earth." The fact that He is king means that there is a kingdom. The fact that there is a kingdom means that there is place or domain of rulership. Jesus is the king of the kingdom of God and He rules over His kingdom.

It's interesting that the writer here said that His rule extends over all the earth. This is why the Psalmist David said in Psalm 24 that "the earth is the Lord's and the fullness thereof." It is also why Jesus taught His disciples to pray "your kingdom come, your will be done, on earth as it is in heaven." We see from these Scriptures alone how that the rule of God is to be demonstrated and manifested throughout the earth.

With this understanding that Christ Jesus is king and that He rules, let's look at Psalm 22:3, "But You are holy, Enthroned in the praises of Israel" (NKJV).

We see in this Scripture that the Lord is enthroned in the praise of His people. A throne is the place that a king executes his rule and domain. It is the place that a king is observed as the supreme ruler.

It is in the middle of our praise that the rule of God is executed. It is our praise that builds a throne for God to come and sit down. Our praise becomes His throne from which He rules with power and strength.

Another Scripture that bears this principle out is Isaiah 16:5, "In mercy the throne will be established; And One will sit on it in truth, in the tabernacle of David, Judging and seeking justice and hastening righteousness" (NKJV).

Here we see clearly stated that He (the Lord) will sit on the throne in the tabernacle of David. Earlier, we discussed the restoration of the tabernacle of David and its significance to the ministry of praise and worship. We saw that God is restoring the tabernacle of David (the ministry of praise and worship) to place a weapon of warfare in our hands.

Here we see that the rule and dominion of God is executed in the tabernacle of David. We see that the throne is established in the tabernacle of David. The Spirit of the Lord is revealing to us that it is in the place of praise and worship that the rule of God will be exercised and manifested.

It's interesting that believers are referred to as "kings and priests" in the book of Revelation. We know that praise is a part of the priestly ministry of every Christian. But then we see this connection between the priestly and kingly ministry of believers. I propose that it is one and the same.

In other words, in the midst of our priestly ministry of praise and worship, the kingly ministry of ruling and reigning is also manifested. It is in the midst of our praise that King Jesus begins to rule through us. It is in the midst of our worship that His throne is established and dominion power is released.

"He will subdue the peoples under us, and the nations under our feet" (Ps. 47:3, NKJV).

The **fifth** principle for effective and powerful praise is simply the understanding that *THROUGH PRAISE WE SUBDUE THE ENEMY.* Since this book has been primarily about the subject of spiritual warfare through praise, I will not go through all the Scriptures and principles of praise as a spiritual weapon. I will just share one verse that I believe has great significance and will bring further understanding.

> *Judah, you are he whom your brothers shall praise; Your hand shall be on the neck of your enemies; Your father's children shall bow down before you* (Gen. 49:8).

Here we see that Judah *(praise)* will have his hand on the neck of his enemies. I believe that this is a prophetic declaration of how praise would be a weapon of spiritual warfare. It is through praise and worship that we can silence the enemy. This revelation will empower our praise to cause damage to the kingdoms of darkness.

The **sixth** principle for effective praise is the understanding that *PRAISE WILL BRING YOU INTO YOUR INHERITANCE.* The Psalmist said "He will choose our inheritance for us." God has an inheritance for everyone who has been redeemed by the blood of Jesus. It is something that has already been given, yet still must be possessed.

The Israelites who came out of Egypt were given a land that flowed with milk and honey. However, only two of them actually took possession. The writer of Hebrews said that all of the other Israelites failed to enter into the land specifically because of unbelief (Heb. 3:19). It was their unbelief that hindered them and prevented them from entering into the inheritance that God had already given them.

With that in mind, we look at the life of Abraham. It is said that, "He did not waver at the promise of God through unbelief, but was strengthened in faith, giving glory to God" (Ro. 4:20). One translation says that Abraham grew strong in faith as he gave glory to God. Abraham's faith was empowered and strengthened as he worshipped the Lord. In other words, Abraham was propelled into his inheritance because of his faith that was empowered by praise.

Interesting enough, Abraham could have wavered and doubted, but he didn't. While he waited on the fulfillment of the promise, he did not doubt or fall into unbelief. The thing we see mentioned specifically in connection to not wavering or falling into unbelief is that Abraham continued to give glory to God. Praise brought Abraham into his inheritance. Hallelujah!

This is a spiritual principle that we all need to grasp today. Praise will cause our inheritance to become a reality within our lives. If we will choose to praise rather than complain, then there will be no opportunity for words of doubt to come out of our mouths. If we will choose to worship rather than worry, then we will give no place to fear and unbelief.

Abraham had to make a choice to give glory to God. He chose to do so even when he didn't feel like it. I'm sure that there were times when everything on the outside was shouting "give up on your inheritance." I'm sure there were times when others did not understand why he had changed his name from Abram to Abraham seeing that *Abraham* means father of many nations and he didn't have a child. Yet, Abraham in the midst of it all, continued to give glory to God.

There are times when you may not feel like praising. There are times that you may not want to lift your hands or begin to rejoice before the Lord. But, I want to encourage you that just like Abraham, your faith can be strengthened as you praise the Lord and that will bring you into your inheritance.

The **last** principle for effective praise is the revelation that *GOD WILL ARISE ON YOUR BEHALF AS YOU PRAISE HIM.*

"God has gone up with a shout, the Lord with the sound of a trumpet" (Psalm 47:5).

The term "gone up" here literally means to be stirred up or arise. So, it is in the midst of praise that God arises. If we want God to arise, then we must begin to give Him glory. The Psalmist said "Let God arise, let His enemies be scattered." God is stirred against our enemy and arises on our behalf when we praise Him.

Understand that God will manifest Himself in the manner that we praise Him. If we praise Him as our Deliverer, then He will arise as Deliverer in our lives. If we praise Him as Healer, then healing will be manifested. If we praise Him as Provider, then our needs will be supplied according to His riches in glory.

So often, people fail to praise God in the area for which they need to see breakthrough. Instead, they complain and talk about the situation. They moan, rather than praise. They groan, rather than worship. It is so easy for Christians to fall into this snare of the enemy.

I encourage you today not to go down that path. Choose to praise and worship regardless of situations and circumstances knowing that God will arise on your behalf when you do. Choose to give Him glory with the understanding that your enemy will be scattered and the victory we have in Christ Jesus will be manifested. Let God arise and His enemies be scattered!

CHAPTER ELEVEN

CRUSHING THE HEAD OF THE SERPENT

We have received a lot of teaching and read numerous books on our position with Christ Jesus and our spiritual authority over the enemy. The Word of God declares that all things are under our feet (1 Cor. 15:25). It also declares that evil principalities and powers are spoiled (Is. 33:1). If all of this is true, why do we have to fight? Why do we have to war against a defeated foe?

First, we must understand the difference between legal position and living reality. Legally and positionally the devil has no authority over any child of God, yet he has caused oppression, sickness and sin. But that does not change the truth of God's Word.

We must learn to acquire that which is legally and positionally ours, bringing it into a living reality that we can experience. The same apostle Paul who wrote that "all things are under your feet" also wrote that we are to fight, war, wrestle and take up weapons of war. Although he wrote that principalities and powers are spoiled, he also wrote that we are still wrestling against them (Eph. 6:12). None of this will make sense to us until we realize the difference between legal position and living reality.

Our spiritual position in Christ Jesus enables us to bring forth the living reality of His victory. Praise, worship, prayer and the Word of God are the tools and weapons we use to bring positional truth into living reality.

In Romans 16:20, Paul writes, "The God of peace will soon crush Satan under your feet" (NIV). As I meditated upon this verse, I began to understand there is a difference between the devil just being under my feet and him being crushed under my feet. I don't want the devil just under my feet; I want him crushed beneath them! How do we crush the devil under our feet?

*"But for you who revere my name, the sun of righteousness will rise with healing in its wings. And you will go out and **leap** like calves released from the stall. Then you will **trample** down the wicked; they will be ashes under the soles of your feet on the day when*

I do these things," says the Lord
Almighty (Mal. 4:2-3, NIV, emphasis
added).

This Scripture verse refers to leaping like
calves released from the stall. This is an
analogy used to describe the way we are to rejoice before the Lord. If you have seen a rodeo,
you can understand this. When the gate of the
stall is opened, the bull jumps and leaps.

Malachi is prophesying that as we begin
to leap and dance before the Lord in praise to
His name, we will trample down the wicked. To
trample something is to put it under our feet.
We don't use our heads or hands to trample. We
trample with our feet. So we trample the
wicked (the devil) under our feet as we go out
and leap like calves released. Webster's dictio-
nary defines *trample* as "to crush as by treading
heavily upon." The devil is crushed beneath our
feet as we go forth with rejoicing and dancing.

Malachi goes on to say that the wicked
"will be ashes under the soles of your feet" (v.
3). From this verse I believe we can see that we
can do spiritual warfare with our feet as we
leap and dance before the Lord. When we dance
before the Lord, there is a purpose for doing so.
We don't dance because it is the charismatic
thing to do. We dance before the Lord because
the Bible tells us to, and we crush the head of
the serpents as we do so. We are dancing in cel-

ebration of the victory that we have won in Christ Jesus. Psalm 149:3 says, "Let them praise his name with dancing" (NIV).

This is not the only method we use to crush the enemy. But dancing and rejoicing are scriptural means by which we can conduct spiritual warfare, thereby bruising the serpent's head.

In Ezekiel 28:11-19, we find a prophecy to Satan. God declares, "I will bring thee to ashes upon the earth" (v. 18). How is God going to bring the devil to ashes? I believe the church is the instrument God is using to accomplish this. According to Malachi 4:2-3, we will make the wicked – the devil – as ashes under our feet, as we go out and leap like calves released from the stall! As we go forth rejoicing and dancing we will see the devil brought to ashes.

Let us look at another Scripture passage concerning the relationship of praise and the treading down of our enemies.

> Mine anger was kindled against the shepherds, and I punished the goats: for the Lord of hosts hath visited his flock the **house of Judah**, and hath made them as his goodly horse in the battle...And they shall be as mighty men, which **tread down their enemies** in the mire of the streets in the battle

and they shall fight, because the Lord
is with them, and the riders on horses
shall be confounded (Zech. 10:3, 5,
emphasis added).

We know the name of Judah means praise.
Thus we see that God will make the people of
praise, the house of Judah, like His royal horse
in the battle. We are the horse that the Lord of
hosts rides into battle. This passage goes on to
state that the Lord and His people of praise will
be like mighty men who tread down their enemies. As we praise God with our feet, they become instruments of war to tread upon the
enemy's head.

For some reason the areas of dance and
expressive worship receive a lot of criticism
from people who do not understand it. Some
have created controversy with terms like
"dancing in the Spirit" versus "dancing in the
flesh." Being from a Pentecostal background, I
understand what is being said. Many Pentecostal churches teach that you are not to dance
before the Lord unless the "Spirit moves you."
To dance deliberately as an act of your will is
considered by many to be "in the flesh."
Choreographed dance is equally thought to be
"in the flesh."

I have never understood exactly why the
feet get picked on. Perhaps it's because the
enemy wants to keep us blinded to the power

109

that is released as God's people praise Him with dancing.

In the book of James, the Bible refers to the tongue as the most defiled member of the body. Yet I have never heard anyone accused of "singing in the flesh!" How do we sing? We look at the words of the song, open our mouths and begin to sing without any prompting by the Holy Spirit. If we can do this with the most defiled member of the body, how much more can we deliberately, as an act of our wills, begin to dance before the Lord?

A religious spirit can cause a critical, judgmental attitude that accuses others of being in the flesh with their worship and praise. These kinds of accusations do not edify the body of Christ; they only foster confusion. God has called us to liberty (2 Cor. 3:17). Michal, Saul's daughter and David's wife, looked out on David as he danced before the Lord and disdained him for it (2 Sam. 6:16). The end result for her was barrenness. Our own lives and ministries can become barren and unfruitful if we look at the praise and worship of others with a critical eye.

Michal was on the wrong side of the window. Instead of looking out on her husband, David, she could have been out there with him. Instead of criticizing, she should have been participating.

We find something very interesting in the account of Gideon's victory over the Midianites. After Gideon and his army blew the trumpets, broke the pitchers and gave up a shout, the Midianite army ran in terror. Some of the Midianite soldiers rose up against each other and killed one another.

> *When the three hundred trumpets sounded, the Lord caused the men throughout the camp to turn on each other with swords. The army fled to Beth Shittah toward Zererah as far as the border of Abel Meholah near Tabbath* (Judg. 7:22, NIV).

The part of the army that fled ran as far as the border of Abel Meholah. In other words, final victory was realized at Abel Meholah. The name *Abel Meholah* means "meadow of the dance." As we go forth dancing and rejoicing before the Lord, our enemy, the devil, is crushed beneath our feet. We, the church, are a great army that is on the offensive. The devil is on the run. Let us pursue him to Abel Mehola and there trample him beneath our feet with rejoicing, dancing and praise!

111

CHAPTER TWELVE

EVERY STROKE WILL BE TO THE MUSIC

The voice of the Lord will shatter
Assyria: with his scepter he will strike
them down. Every stroke the Lord lays
on them with his punishing rod will be
to the music of tambourines and harps,
as he fights them in battle with the
blows of his arm (Is. 30:31-32, NIV).

What a powerful Scripture passage! In
this chapter I would like to examine the role of
prophetic music in spiritual warfare. We have
been taught that prophecy edifies, exhorts and
comforts. We've had similar teaching that
anointed music can minister to both the soul
and spirit of a man. I believe that God wants us
to see that the prophetic voice of the Lord and
anointed prophetic music are weapons of war to
be used against our enemy. When God called
Jeremiah, He said,

Now, I have put my words in your
mouth. See, today I appoint you over

*nations and kingdoms to uproot and
tear down, to destroy and overthrow,
to build and to plant.* (Jer. 1:9-10,
NIV).

Notice that four of the six things the word
of the Lord will do are destructive. The
prophetic word comes not only to edify and exhort us, but also to uproot, tear down, destroy
and overthrow the kingdom of darkness. The
same word that blesses us destroys the enemy.
The prophetic word has power to destroy the
works of the enemy. That's why Paul told
Timothy to war a good warfare with the prophe-
cies spoken over him (Tim 1:18). Obviously,
Paul had a revelation of using the prophetic
word in spiritual warfare.

With this in mind, let's look at the prophetic
song.

*Do not get drunk on wine which leads
to debauchery. Instead be filled with
the Spirit. Speak to one another with
psalms, hymns and spiritual songs.
Sing and make music in your heart to
the Lord, always giving thanks to God
the Father for everything, in the name
of the Lord Jesus Christ* (Eph. 5:18-20,
NIV).

Paul lists three different categories of
songs: psalms, hymns and spiritual songs. I

would like to focus on the last one – *spiritual songs*. The literal definition of a spiritual song is "ode of the Spirit" or "song of the Spirit." These are songs of praise, prophecy, warfare, healing and deliverance. They are prophetic in nature in the same sense that they come forth spontaneously in an inspirational manner. They are also prophetic in the sense that God is singing through His church, expressing His mind, purpose and will. I can see six different types of prophetic or spiritual songs found in the Bible. I would like to discuss each one individually, paying particular attention to the last two.

SONG OF THE LORD

The **first** is called the song of the Lord (2 Chron. 29:27). The song of the Lord is, literally, prophecy in song. It is "thus says the Lord" coming forth through a song. It has the same purpose as prophecy, which is to edify, exhort and comfort (1 Cor.14:3).

The Lord thy God in the midst of thee is mighty; he will save, he will rejoice over thee with joy; he will rest in his love, he will joy over thee with singing (Zeph. 3:17).

This reveals that the Lord will rejoice over us with singing. Many do not realize that

114

our God sings. He desires to sing to His church. In Psalm 91 we have an example of the song of the Lord. In the beginning of this psalm, the psalmist praises the Lord and declares that God is our fortress. But as he reaches the end of the psalm, the person singing changes.

"Because he loves me," says the Lord, "I will rescue him; I will protect him, for he acknowledges my name. He will call upon me, and I will answer him; I will be with him in trouble, I will deliver him and honor him. With long life will I satisfy him and show him my salvation" (Ps.91:14-16, NIV).

Notice that it says, "'Because he loves me,' says the Lord." The psalmist begins by singing to the Lord, but the Lord ends the psalm by singing to the psalmist. God declares prophetically to the psalmist through song what He will do. It is the Lord singing to His people.

SONG OF THE LORD (DIRECTED TO THE FATHER)

The **second** type of prophetic song is also the song of the Lord, but it is directed to the Father rather than to the church. This is an inspired prophetic song of praise, worship and adoration. Some call this the singing of a new song.

*He says, "I will declare your name to
my brothers; in the presence of the
congregation I will sing your praises"*
(Heb. 2:12, NIV).

The verse refers to Jesus as He sings
praise to the Father in the midst of the congregation. How will He do this? He will do this
through His body, the church.

THE SONG OF THE BRIDEGROOM

The **third** type of prophetic song is called
the song of the bridegroom. In Revelation 19:7
the Bible refers to the church as the bride. The
bridegroom is Jesus. We have a beautiful picture of the song of the bridegroom painted in
the Song of Solomon. Most Bible scholars will
agree that the Song of Solomon typifies the relationship between Christ and His church.

We see a picture of the bridegroom sere-
nading His bride. The song of the bridegroom is
much like the song of the Lord but is usually a
love song to the bride and is then followed by
the song of the bride.

*In the towns of Judah and the streets
of Jerusalem that are deserted, inhab-
ited by neither men nor animals,
there will be heard once more the
sounds of joy and gladness, **the voices***

116

of bride and bridegroom, and the voices of those who bring thank offerings to the house of the Lord saying, "Give thanks to the Lord Almighty, for the Lord is good; His love endures forever" (Jer. 33:10-11, NIV, emphasis added).

SONG OF THE BRIDE

This brings us to the **fourth** type of prophetic song called the song of the bride. This is a spontaneous prophetic song of love and adoration in response to the song of the bridegroom. This type of prophetic song is usually responsive in nature as the bride expresses to the bridegroom her love for Him. It is also usually intimate in nature and enables the church to express by the Spirit of God the depth of love it has for the bridegroom, Jesus.

SONG OF DELIVERANCE

The **fifth** type of prophetic song is called the song of deliverance. This is a prophetic song of healing, deliverance and restoration. It is much like a word of knowledge in song.

Thou art my hiding place; thou shalt preserve me from trouble; thou shalt compass me about with songs of deliverance (Ps. 32:7).

117

This type of song releases instantaneous manifestations of healing, miracles and deliverance. It is where the voice of the Lord, through song, begins to destroy the work of the enemy.

In June 1988, I was ministering in a Sunday evening service in Griffin, Georgia. After teaching on praise and worship I began to play the keyboard and lead the church in worship. As we worshipped, I sensed the Spirit of God prompting me to sing a song of deliverance. I mustered up enough faith and stepped out and sang, "there is someone here who was in an accident and misaligned the vertebrae in your neck. You have continual pain in that area. But now the hand of the Lord is upon you and you are being set free and healed by the power of God."

I wasn't sure if I was right or not. I was acting on a slight impression of what I sensed in my spirit. At the end of the service, a woman in the back of the auditorium came to the front and shared with the pastor's wife what happened to her. She later told me the same story.

"I was in an automobile accident," she said, "and misaligned some vertebrae in my neck. I had continual pain to the point of having to take heavy medication to be able to cope. As you began to sing that song, it felt like warm hands were placed on the back of my neck. Something popped in my neck, and every bit of pain left me instantaneously."

The pastor was in one of our conferences later that year in October. We were riding in a van together when he asked me if I recalled that service with the lady who was healed. I told him "yes." He said that the lady had experienced no pain since that night. Hallelujah! The voice of the Lord shattered the work of the enemy. The song of deliverance had accomplished its purpose. It brought healing and deliverance from the oppression of the enemy.

PROPHETIC SONG OF WAR

The **sixth** and last type of prophetic song is called the prophetic song of war. This song declares our victory in Christ Jesus. Its purpose is to wage spiritual warfare against principalities, powers, rulers of the darkness of this world and spiritual wickedness in the heavenly realms. It is directed toward our enemy and at times will even call out the name of a particular demonic power. It is a prophecy that is sung to demonic forces.

> *And you will **sing** as on the night you celebrate a holy festival; **your hearts will** rejoice as when people go up with flutes to the mountain of the Lord, to the Rock of Israel. The Lord will cause men to hear his majestic voice and will make them see his arm coming down with raging anger and consuming fire, with cloudburst, thunderstorm and*

*hail. The **voice of the Lord will shatter Assyria**; with his scepter he will strike them down. Every stroke the Lord lays on them with his punishing rod **will be to the music of tambourines and harps, as he fights them in battle with the blows of his arm*** (Is. 30:29-32, NIV, emphasis added).

This passage records that the Lord causes His voice to be heard in the midst of singing and rejoicing: "You will sing," and "your hearts will rejoice." In the midst of praise, God will "cause men to hear His majestic voice."

Then Isaiah tells us what the voice of the Lord will do. "The voice of the Lord will shatter Assyria [the enemy]." As you read these verses together, you see a picture of God's voice being released through the prophetic song.

Let's explore this a little more. The King James Version reads like this: "For through the voice of the Lord shall the Assyrian be beaten down." Then Isaiah says by the Spirit of God that "every stroke...will be to the music" (v. 32, NIV). In other words, the prophetic voice of the Lord strikes and beats down the enemy as it is administered through music (or song).

He is talking about the prophetic song. The word "beaten" is the Hebrew word *chathath*. It means "to prostrate" or "to break down by violence or by confusion and fear."

This is what Isaiah declares the voice of the Lord will do. As we sing prophetically, strokes are laid upon our enemy. We bring confusion to the camp of the enemy through the prophetic song. Demonic forces are terrorized as we declare in song what the Spirit of God is saying.

I recall a particular service in which I was leading worship. It seemed as if no one was entering into the praise. Something seemed to be binding the people from praise. There was no liberty or freedom. I asked the Lord what to do. I sensed Him telling me to sing prophetically.

"But, Lord, I don't have anything to sing prophetically," I replied.

"Open your mouth, and I will fill it," I heard the Lord say.

So I opened my mouth, and sang, "For the Spirit of the Lord would say," and I proceeded to sing a prophetic song. Words flowed forth from my spirit as I acted in faith on what God had spoken to me. As the prophetic song came forth, the binding spirit was "beaten down." Freedom came into the service. The worship service ended with everyone praising the Lord with wild abandonment. It was glorious.

When God took Ezekiel to the valley of dry bones (Ezek. 37), Ezekiel saw the power of the prophetic word. God spoke to Ezekiel to prophesy to the bones. As he prophesied to them, the bones came on them, and they stood up. He then prophesied for the wind to blow upon them, and they came forth as a great army. The prophetic word of the Lord has **resurrection power!** You may think your congregation is dead, but I guarantee that it's not as dead as Ezekiel's congregation was that day. The word of the Lord can breathe life into your worship service.

In another service Dr. Bill Hamon called a special warfare praise and intercession service at Christian International. The ministry had come under the attack of a major principality. Jane Hamon, co pastor of the Christian International Family Church, had prophetically received the name of the principality that was bringing the attack against us. The name was *Rahabar.*

At one point in the praise and worship we said corporately, "Rahabar, you are bound, and now you're coming down." We repeated this statement over and over with vehemence as the music played and then ended with a victory shout. The attack of the enemy ceased. The enemy was stopped in his tracks as we recited prophetically and sang to this principality with a revelation of what we were accomplishing.

Paul spoke of this in the third chapter of Ephesians:

*His intent was that now, through the
church, the manifold wisdom of God
should be made known to the rulers
and authorities in the heavenly realms*
(Eph. 3:10, NIV).

Notice that it is through the church that
the wisdom of God, or His word, is to be made
known to the rulers in the heavenly realms.
God has given us, the church, the responsibility
of declaring His word prophetically to demonic
powers and principalities for the purpose of destroying their kingdom.

Let's look at the familiar story of David
and Goliath. As David went out to meet the
Philistine giant, he said to him:

*You come against me with sword and
spear and javelin, but I come against
you in the name of the Lord Almighty,
the God of the armies of Israel, whom
you have defied. This day the Lord will
hand you over to me, and I'll strike
you down and cut off your head. Today
I will give the carcasses of the
Philistine army to the birds of the air
and the beasts of the earth, and the
whole world will know that there is a
God in Israel. All those gathered here
will know that it is not by sword or
spear that the Lord saves; for the*

battle is the Lord's, and he will give all of you into our hands (1 Sam. 17:45-47, NIV).

I do not believe this was a faith confession. I believe something rose up inside David, and he began to prophesy to the giant. Notice he said, "This day..." David got specific. There is no margin for error when you get that specific. But I thank God that David had the word of the Lord for the giant.

The Philistine giant is a type of the enemy we face. God wants us to arise and prophesy to the demonic "bully" that is trying to push us around. Even though the battle was the Lord's, David still had to go out and face the giant, sling the stone and cut off his head. God causes us to triumph, but, like David, *we must go out and fight!*

We can derive another mighty truth from this story. As David declared, "The whole world will know that there is a God in Israel." When would the world know? After he slayed Goliath! Do you know when the world is going to know there is a God in the church? When we arise in the power of the Spirit, as the great and mighty army that Ezekiel prophesied about, and slay the spiritual giants that are trying to rule the earth.

We must remind ourselves that people do not believe in Jesus because they have been blinded by demonic spirits (2 Cor. 4:4). Spiritual warfare should precede the preaching of the Word; people will be saved when they are no longer blinded by evil spirits.

A New Testament example of this is found in the book of Acts. Paul and Barnabas had traveled to the island of Cyprus. Upon reaching the island they traveled from one end to the other. Arriving in the city of Paphos, they met a Jewish sorcerer and false prophet named Bar-jesus. This man was an attendant of the proconsul Sergius Paulus. The proconsul wanted to hear the gospel, so he sent for Paul and Barnabas. Bar-Jesus was obviously not thrilled about this and opposed Paul and Barnabas.

> *Then Saul, (who also is called Paul,) filled with the Holy Ghost, set his eyes on him, and said, O full of all subtlety and all mischief, thou child of the devil, thou enemy of all righteousness, wilt thou not cease to pervert the right ways of the Lord? And now, behold, the hand of the Lord is upon thee, and thou shalt be blind, not seeing the sun for a season. And immediately there fell on him a mist and darkness; and he went about seeking some to lead him by the hand. Then the deputy, when he saw what was done, believed, being astonished at the doctrine of the Lord* (Acts 13:9-12).

Bar-jesus represents the spirits of false religion and antichrist. Paul looks at him and prophesies the word of the Lord to him. The Spirit of God arose with Paul, and he pronounced a prophetic judgment upon Bar-jesus.

Again, we see the principle of prophesying to demonic principalities and powers. This man, Bar-jesus, was practicing the same thing that the many false prophets posing as talk-show hosts and journalists are propagating today. We can expect to see some of the same things happen to them that happened to Bar-jesus.

I would like you to see the results of this prophetic word: "Then the deputy when he saw what was done, believed" (v.12). Paul's prophetic declaration resulted in a demonstration of the power of God which made a believer out of the deputy. He knew that almighty God was with Paul. Recall what David said to Goliath: "I am going to kill you today and 'the whole world will know that there is a God in Israel."

Another example of prophesying to wicked principalities and powers is found in Exodus 5. Pharaoh is a type of the enemy that holds people in bondage.

And afterward Moses and Aaron went in, and told Pharaoh, Thus saith the

126

> *Lord God of Israel, Let my people go,
> that they may hold a feast unto me in
> the wilderness* (Ex. 5:1).

Here we see Moses and Aaron going before Pharaoh and giving him the word of the Lord. I am giving all these scriptural examples to establish the validity of the principle of prophesying to demonic powers. Many times in our worship services, we have sung prophetically to demonic principalities. In these songs, we executed the judgment that was written upon them (Ps. 149:9).

We have seen great things happen as a result of the prophetic songs of war. At times, these songs come forth in an antiphonal, or responsive, manner. Military squads march to antiphonal singing. The word "antiphonal" is derived from two words: *anti* and *phonal*. *Anti* means "against," and *phonal* means "sound." In prophetic antiphonal singing, we literally sound against the principalities and powers of the air.

God desires to speak, and He wants His voice to be heard. The apostle Paul said, "Covet to prophesy" (1 Cor. 14:39). The Spirit of God would not have conveyed this through Paul if it were something we could not do. Let us release the voice of the Lord through the prophetic song. The church will be edified and blessed, and the kingdom of darkness will be terrorized and depressed. Let us move into the prophetic song with confidence and faith, realizing that God's Spirit will be released with power as we do so.

CHAPTER THIRTEEN

THE SONGS OF PROPHETIC WARFARE

Every move of God has produced new songs and choruses that declare what is being preached and taught. We are in the midst of an apostolic and prophetic move of God. He is bringing forth in this hour a great company of apostles and prophets. Along with this, the saints of God are arising with the power of God to demonstrate to this generation. There is a company of prophetic songwriters that are arising to pen in song that which the Lord is saying today. Spiritual warfare is one of the messages that the Spirit of the God is declaring and releasing in the earth.

I believe in having a purpose for everything I do. Without it I accomplish nothing. When I first began writing songs, I wrote aimlessly. I would write whatever came to me in moments of inspiration. As I continued, the Lord was faithful in teaching me how to write. He also spoke to me about stirring up the prophetic songwriting gift within me. Since then I've written several hundred songs.

One of the questions that I have been asked from time to time is "Why do we need to sing aggressive, confrontational, militant songs? Why can't we just sing sweet songs about the love of Jesus?" These are valid questions which I will try to answer from the Bible and give some personal experiences and observations.

Colossians chapter three contains the first two purposes for warfare songs:

> Let the word of Christ dwell in you richly in all wisdom; teaching and admonishing one another in psalms and hymns and spiritual songs, singing with grace in your hearts to the Lord (Col. 3:16).

The **first** purpose is to teach us biblical truth about spiritual warfare. Warfare music usually contains verses that speak of spiritual warfare, including some that may be unfamiliar. They declare our victory in Jesus Christ, while at the same time making us aware that we are still wrestling and fighting against demonic forces. Warfare songs speak of the army of the Lord going out to battle against our enemy. An army's purpose is to fight.

Warfare songs may challenge a person's religious indoctrination. Every warfare song I have written can be validated with numerous Scripture verses. We should first investigate the whole Word of God, not just selected verses.

A **second** purpose for warfare music is to admonish one another. The word *admonish* means "to put in mind." In other words, once we are established in the truth of spiritual warfare, we then stir up our remembrance as we sing our songs. We put these truths in our minds through the singing of warfare songs. Notice what Peter said:

> Wherefore I will not be negligent to put you always in remembrance of these things, though you know them, and be established in the present truth (2 Peter 1:12).

Once you are established in the present truth of spiritual warfare and warfare praise, you must still have your memory stirred up. Singing of warfare songs accomplishes this.

A **third** purpose for warfare songs is to exhort. To *exhort* in the Greek means "to call near" or "to call for." It also means "to give a charge." As we sing these songs, we call for the army of the Lord to come forth. We call near all the warriors.

> *Proclaim this among the nations:*
> *Prepare for war! Rouse the warriors!*
> *Let all the fighting men draw near and*
> *attack* (Joel 3:9, NIV).

We, the church, are not a social club. We are an army that is at war against the devil and his demonic forces. An army assembles its troops.

I know of many intercession groups that play prophetic warfare tapes before they pray. The music stirs them up to war in the spirit. Thus we see how warfare music exhorts.

The **fourth** purpose for warfare songs is to release people in praise to the Lord. One of the main Hebrew words translated "praise" is *halal*. This word means "to declare, to make a show, boast, to be clamorously foolish." When we sing a song such as "Mighty Man of War," we declare that our God is a warrior. That is praising the Lord. Songs that speak of our victory in Christ or of overcoming the devil are praise to the Lord.

When we say the word "praise," most people think of the book of Psalms. It is very interesting to read some of the psalms that the warrior David wrote by the Spirit of God. Some of those psalms praise God for killing wicked kings – even calling them by name!

Many of the psalms contain statements that beseech the Lord to destroy people, break their teeth, cut off their seed, strike people with terror, clothe them with shame or bring coals upon their heads. The warfare songs we have written today are actually mild compared to some that David wrote. Yet no one would dispute that those psalms can be used to praise the Lord.

Warfare songs praise the Lord. God is glorified as we sing what is contained in His Word. Songs do not have to be vertical songs – those directed toward God – to be praise to Him. Songs that speak of who we are as the army of the Lord and what that army is doing are praise.

A **fifth** purpose for warfare songs is that they unite us against a common enemy. During the Gulf War and Operation Desert Storm unity in the United States seemed to be high. A common enemy and a common goal will always rally and unite people. We are exposing the enemy as we sing warfare songs. Instead of using the sword on our brothers or sister, we realize that our swords have the devil's name on the blade.

Although the United States and the former USSR were diametrically opposed to each other, they became allies against Nazi Germany during World War II. When a common enemy exists, differences no longer matter. During the Gulf War in 1992, we witnessed a nation considered to be predominantly Christian – the USA – join forces with several Islamic nations to fight against another Islamic nation – Iraq. The only thing that made this possible was the common-enemy principle. As we, the church, come into this revelation of a common enemy, we will see greater unity and victory. Warfare songs play a key role in developing this unity.

A **sixth** purpose for warfare songs is the release of corporate warfare.

That the communication of thy faith may become effectual by the acknowledging of every good thing which is in you in Christ Jesus (Philem. 6).

I believe the key phrase in this verse is "may become effectual by the acknowledging." The acknowledging of biblical truths causes them to become effective. That is a spiritual principle that applies even to salvation. It is the acknowledging of Jesus as Lord that causes salvation to become effective in the heart of the believer (Rom. 10:9-10).

As we corporately acknowledge the Lord as a warrior, that character attribute of God becomes effective in our lives. He rises in us as the mighty warrior. Along with that, in the spirit realm angelic beings go forth and fight as they hearken to the "voice of His word" (Ps. 103:20).

As we acknowledge the warfare taking place in the spirit realm, our spiritual warfare through praise becomes more effective. The power of God is released in the heavenlies, pulling down strongholds and scattering demonic principalities.

The last purpose for warfare songs is to declare in song what the Holy Spirit is saying to the church. In the prophetic movement, the church has figuratively crossed over the Jordan and entered the promised land. Jordan has rolled back behind us, and there is nowhere to go but forward! The manna has ceased, and now we must go milk the cows and rob the beehives in order to have milk and honey.

The prophets are calling for the army of the Lord to come forth. The prophetic words are declaring that we, the church, must take up our weapons of war and fight.

I have purposed in my heart to write what the Spirit of God is declaring today. He wants us to sing forth His words. As we do, we will see the release of God's power and anointing through the church and the destruction of the kingdom of darkness.

SYNOPSIS:

ADVANCE AND OCCUPY

We have repeatedly seen how praise is used as a weapon of warfare. Throughout God's Word the Spirit of God demonstrated to us that praise and worship are more than words and music. Our praise has power to destroy and demolish the kingdom of darkness.

What is written and declared in the Bible is there for our admonition and instruction. The accounts that we read are there for us to follow. God has given the church a powerful weapon of war. That weapon is the high praises of God in our mouths.

It is time for the church to arise out of passivity and move into a dimension of militancy against the powers of hell. With the praises of God on our lips we take possession of what God has declared is already ours. We drive out the demonic principalities that have subjugated our rightful possessions and proceed to advance and occupy our land.

136

With our praise we silence the enemy. His plans fail as he lacks the power to carry them out. Uninhibited worship torments the enemy of our soul. The joyful sound of praise causes shock waves to be felt throughout the kingdom of darkness.

With our praise we execute the vengeance of our God upon the head of our enemy the devil. The principalities and powers that Jesus spoiled are bound with chains and with fetters of iron (Ps. 149:8). The judgments that almighty God has declared in His Word are enforced as His glorious praise goes forth.

Our plowshares are beaten into swords as we receive the revelation of the Spirit. Our praise then becomes a mighty sword we wield against our foe. No longer do we worship without purpose, but we worship with a revelation of the power of our praise. We sing with purpose and authority while understanding who we are as the body of Christ.

In the midst of our praise, the mighty man of war arises. He fights with us as we extol the greatness of His name. His zeal is stirred against our enemies as we shout joyfully to Him. He marches out to battle, like a warrior sounding the battle cry, as the sound of exaltation comes forth from His people.

Jesus is the Lion of the tribe of Judah. His roar is being heard today as He announces

His victory over the enemy. The devil is terrified at the sound of the roar of God in the earth. The Lord is declaring that victory is ours as the Lion of Judah roars.

God has declared that He inhabits the praises of His people. His presence is manifested in the midst of a worshipping priesthood of believers. He has revealed Himself throughout His Word as the Lord of hosts. He is the Lord of warriors. This mighty warrior is enthroned in our praises. In that habitation of praise He fights with and for us.

Every expression of our praise has a purpose. Every act of praise affects the realm of the spirit. For every action there is an equal and corresponding reaction in the unseen realm. We are not just making a lot of noise.

As we shout to God with the voice of triumph, God arises and His enemies are scattered. Satan's strongholds are broken up. The kingdom of darkness is marred by the high praises of God that are released with shouts of joy.

Confusion and destruction are released into the enemy's camp as we go forth singing the songs of Zion. As Jehoshaphat and the people went out singing about the mercy of God, God's mercy was manifested in the destruction of their enemy. Likewise, as we sing with revelation, God manifests that revelation in our lives.

God is the creator of music. He is the original designer of musical instruments. His most beautiful angel, Lucifer, was created with musical instruments built into his body. Because of pride, Lucifer fell, and his music became perverted. The responsibility of filling the heavenlies with anointed music is now in the hands of the church. David, the man after God's own heart, created a multitude of musical instruments. As we play upon musical instruments in praise and honor of our Lord, the force of God's anointing and power is released, causing the enemy to run in terror.

God's voice is released and heard through prophecy as people praise Him. For every acceptable sacrifice of praise there is always a divine response. God responds to our worship by speaking to us by way of the prophetic word. God's voice is often released through the prophetic song as He rejoices over us with singing. The enemies of God are shattered as His mighty voice is heard. Healing, deliverance and restoration take place as the prophetic song is brought forth.

It is time for us to sing the war songs of Zion. The church has not been called to sit idly among our blessings, but rather to raise up a standard against the forces of darkness. We have been called to show forth His praises. Our songs should reflect our militant stand against the devil. As we sing strong, militant, warfare songs, corporate warfare is released in the heavenly realms. We admonish one another to be strong in the Lord and fight the good fight of faith.

This is not the day to retreat. This is the day to advance. We are not just holding on, but we are possessing. We will not just survive, but we are taking over. We are subduing the kingdom of darkness by declaring the kingdom of God. Let us take up all the weaponry that God has laid at our disposal, including the weapon of praise. We have been called to the kingdom for such an hour as this to silence the enemy.

NOTES

CHAPTER 8

1. Bill Hamon, *Prophets and the Prophetic Movement* (Shippensburg, Pa.: Destiny Image Publishers, 1990).

For more information about books,
music and teaching CDs
by Robert Gay, contact:

High Praise Worship Center
7124 E. Hwy. 22
Panama City, FL 32404
(850) 874-9745
www.highpraiseworshipcenter.com

Parsons Publishing House

Your Voice Your World™

70 REASONS FOR SPEAKING IN TONGUES
by Dr. Bill Hamon

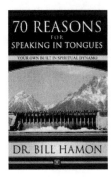

Over 600 million Christians have received the Holy Spirit gift of tongues, and 95% of Spirit-baptized Christians only utilize 10% of the benefits of speaking in tongues. Learn how to use your spirit language to activate more faith and increase God's love and power within your life and ministry (216 pages). $14.95.

Available at your local bookstore.
www.ParsonsPublishingHouse.com